30p

THE PHILHELLENES

By the same author

RHODES (with J. G. Lockhart)
THE BATTLE OF NAVARINO

THE PHILHELLENES

by

C. M. WOODHOUSE

HODDER AND STOUGHTON

First printed 1969
SBN 340 10824 X

Printed in Great Britain for Hodder and Stoughton Limited, St. Paul's House, Warwick Lane, London, E.C.4, by Ebenezer Baylis and Son Limited, The Trinity Press, Worcester, and London

CONTENTS

THE PLATES

[1] The Trustees of the National Portrait Gallery.
[2] The Radio Times Hutton Picture Library.
[3] Taken from *Sir Richard Church in Italy and Greece*, by E. M. Church (Edinburgh 1895).

PREFACE

PHILHELLENISM was a phenomenon of the second and third decades of the 19th century. Because of the pre-eminent personality of Byron, it has not generally been seen in a sufficiently wide context. The philhellenes were more than Byron plus an entourage of eccentrics, ruffians and romantics, though there were plenty of all three. They were part of an international movement of protest in which nationalism, religion, radicalism and commercial greed all played a part, as well as romantic sentiment and pure heroism. This book is an attempt to widen the context.

First, there is the international range of the philhellenes. They came not only from the British Isles (in particular, from Scotland and Ireland), but also from France, Switzerland, Denmark, Italy, Poland, many of the German states, and the United States of America. Their nationalities alone show that philhellenism was part of the liberal movement which succeeded the Napoleonic Wars. In most cases it also follows that the volunteers who took part in the Greek War of Independence had not the approval of the governments which exercised sovereignty over them. Some of those governments were more or less tolerant – the British and French, for example. Others strongly disapproved: the hard core of the Holy Alliance – the Russian, Austrian and Prussian courts – had little sympathy with the volunteers, since whichever side their rulers took in the war was a matter of power politics, not of sentiment.

To some extent, therefore, the philhellene movement was linked with the internal politics of the countries from which the volunteers came. This was the case, for example, with the French, who included both royalists and Buonapartists, bringing their intrigues with them;

and with the Bavarians, whose future King, Ludwig, was something of an imperialist as well as a fanatical philhellene. It was not the case with the Swiss, the Americans, or the minor German nationalities, who were wholly disinterested. With the British, however, the situation was more complicated. The philhellenes in the field were mostly unselfish, but behind them were more powerful forces. One, of course, was the British government, which had acquired the Ionian Islands with their wholly Greek population in 1814, and did not intend to let them go. Another was the political force of radicalism, which took many forms and used all of them as instruments for harassing the Tory government. These forces define another of the enlarged dimensions in which the story of philhellenism must be seen.

There is also a wider chronological setting to be seen. Before the flame was lit by Byron and again after it was extinguished, although there was some interest in Greece, there was no philhellenism. Various causes evoked the interest: classical education, the Grand Tour, the antiquities brought back by the tourists; and also a strategic concern for the eastern Mediterranean, directed first against France and later against Russia. But there was little interest in the Greeks as people. Their connection with the classical Greeks was denied, their language was ridiculed and even the fact that they were a Christian people under heathen rule stirred little emotion, since their Christianity was adjudged even more depraved than that of Rome. Byron and his companions briefly conquered such prejudice and indifference, but they soon flourished again. These too are a necessary part of the story. Not only who the philhellenes were is important, but who they were not.

The identification of them and what they did, though not always why they did it, has been the subject of previous works. Outstanding is Mr. Douglas Dakin's *British and American Philhellenes* (Thessaloniki, 1955). More limited accounts are Mr. Z. D. Ferriman's *Some English Philhellenes* (London, 1917), which covers only the more prominent names, and Mr. Stephen A. Larrabee's *Hellas Observed* (New York, 1957), which comprehensively covers the Americans.

It would be useful to study other groups on a national basis, particularly the French, the Germans and the Swiss. If the present work is confined to the British, it is for two good reasons. One is that there is a particular and unusual interest in the relationship of the British philhellenes to the social and political history of their times, which has not been examined before. The other, which it would be false patriotism to deny, is the predominance, both in numbers and in decisive effect, of the British contingent. No other country can parade even one rival, let alone an equal number, to match the roles played by half a dozen of the British. The names of Lord Byron, Sir Richard Church, Sir Edward Codrington, Captain Frank Abney Hastings, George Finlay and George Canning, are immortal in Greece; and rightly so. Only their fellow-countrymen fail to appreciate their services to the first of the new nation-states to achieve independence in the 19th century. This is an attempt to revive the record and set it straight.

CHAPTER I

The Forerunners

THE TURN OF the year 1809 to 1810 was a gala season in the history of Athens. Something more than a village, but much less than the great city it had once been, Athens was a provincial town of some cultural pretensions, and a minor seat of Turkish misgovernment under the Ottoman Empire. It was already famous among visiting foreigners for its history and ancient monuments. The monuments had been damaged by centuries of Ottoman neglect, followed by the more systematic attentions of the agents of the Earl of Elgin since 1801. Elgin had acquired the post of British Ambassador at Constantinople, the Ottoman capital, in 1799 at the age of 33. As a reward for the British victory over Napoleon in Egypt, he had been awarded a *firman* or authorisation by the Sultan to make copies of the sculptures on the Acropolis – but not, at least on the face of it, to remove them. His agents had already been at work, for several years: in particular the Rev. Philip Hunt and the Italian artist, Giovanni Batista Lusieri.

Their activities had attracted other western Europeans to Athens. Most of them were critical of what Lord Elgin was doing. The "dilapidating mania", it was called by the eminent scholar, Edward Dodwell. Even Lusieri thought it "a little barbarous". The Rev. E. D. Clarke, a mineralogist from Cambridge, who had at one time served under Elgin, did not at all approve the removal of the sculptures which were to become famous as the Elgin Marbles. Nor did the natives, of whom Edward Dodwell later wrote:[1]

"... nor have I any hesitation in saying, that the Athenians in general, nay, even the Turks themselves, did lament the ruin that

[1] *Dodwell, A Classical and Topographical Tour through Greece* (London, 1819), pp. 291, 322–3.

was committed; and loudly and openly blamed their sovereign for the permission he had granted!"

Many other voices were raised against Lord Elgin's depredations, which were only later to be defended on the grounds that he had saved the Marbles from destruction. Lord Byron, who possessed the most eloquent voice of all, had not yet arrived; but in December 1809 he was on his way.

Athens in 1809 had begun to attract new kinds of travellers. Antiquarians and scholars from ancient universities were already familiar to the Athenians. So were holders of official appointments, such as M. Fauvel, the cultivated and popular French Consul, who was deeply jealous of Lord Elgin's agents because he regarded himself as having a monopoly of expertise in the field of antiquities. The British government had not thought it worthwhile to appoint a Consul from England, but the post of Vice-Consul had been entrusted to a Greek called Makris whose daughter, Theodora, was to be immortalised by Byron:

Maid of Athens, ere we part,
Give, Oh give me back my heart!

Other visitors on official business called occasionally in Athens, such as Colonel W. M. Leake, the distinguished geographer, who carried out an exhaustively thorough survey of Greece in the interests of the British government, working against the French during the Napoleonic Wars; and French officers, who performed the same office in reverse.

There was something special, however, about the years 1809–1810. Many observers remarked that visitors were especially thick on the ground. One of the travellers, the Hon. F. S. N. Douglas, a student of Christ Church, Oxford, observed[1] that Greece had been neglected by English travellers until the Napoleonic Wars had shut out most of the continent and directed their love of travel into a new channel. J. C. Hobhouse, who was travelling at the same date with Byron,

[1] Douglas, *An Essay on Certain Points of Resemblance between the Ancient and Modern Greeks* (London, 1813). pp. 6–7.

confirms the same point. "Until within a few years, a journey to Athens was reckoned a considerable undertaking, fraught with difficulties and dangers," he wrote;[1] but "Attica at present swarms with travellers." Dodwell also remarked (in 1813) on the "multiplicity of travellers" exploring Greece in recent years.[2] The proliferation of travel-books recording their experiences is very marked in the first twenty years of the century; and the middle years were the most striking of all.

Byron and Hobhouse reached Athens on Christmas Day 1809, bringing with them a reputation for adventurous travel. They had visited Ali Pasha, the tyrant of Epirus, at his romantic and blood-stained court in Ioannina. They had reflected on the battle of Actium in the vicinity of Preveza. Without foreboding, they had stayed two nights at Mesolonghi, where Byron was to die fifteen years later. At Delphi, they had found carved on a marble column the name of Byron's elder school-fellow, the Earl of Aberdeen, a future Foreign Secretary and Prime Minister. ("There is something agreeable," wrote Hobhouse,[3] "in meeting even with the name of a countryman.") The two young gentlemen were already bored with each other's company when they reached Athens. Hobhouse enthused over the antiquities; Byron detested enthusiasm, and preferred swimming and other sports to pottering round ancient ruins. Hobhouse despised the Greeks, like most Englishmen of the day. It was fashionable, indeed, to claim that they were not really Greeks at all. Byron formed other views, and later gave his life for them; but he liked it to be known that he was their superior, as indeed he was of everybody else.

They were not the first or the only British visitors to Athens that winter. Aristocrats on the Grand Tour, whose glory reflected on all English tourists and conferred on them indiscriminately the title of *lordoi* or "milords", were already plentiful. There was Lady Hester Stanhope, the niece of William Pitt, who left England for ever after

[1] Hobhouse, *A Journey through Albania and other Provinces of Turkey in Europe and Asia to Constantinople during the years 1809 and 1810*, 2nd ed. (London, 1813), vol. I, pp. 301–2.

[2] Dodwell, p. iii.

[3] Hobhouse, vol. I, p. 247.

his death in 1806, and paused awhile in Athens on her way to becoming a legend in Syria. Among the grand tourists later in the year 1810 were the young Marquess of Sligo, the Hon. Frederick North, and his cousin, the Hon. F. S. N. Douglas. North was the son of the Prime Minister who had lost the American colonies. Douglas was a student of Christ Church – that is to say, an Oxford don—and a future M.P. With him were two other young gentlemen combining antiquariansim with the Grand Tour: J. H. Fazakerly, also a future M.P. and a colleague of Douglas on the Select Committee of Parliament on the Elgin Marbles in 1816; and H. G. Knight, later well-known as an architectural scholar, whose "oriental poems" won the interest of Byron himself. On a lower social scale, there was a young poet, William Haygarth, who was not to know that his *Greece, a poem in three parts, with notes, classical illustrations, and sketches of the scenery*, would be eclipsed by a greater genius among his contemporary travellers. There was John Galt, a Scottish novelist, engaged in collecting what he called[1] "statistical, commercial and miscellaneous observations," and also helping the Earl of Elgin's agents in removing the Parthenon Marbles. There was a distinguished antiquarian, C. R. Cockerell, who made many archælogical discoveries of the first importance. Among the mere tourists, whose one claim to fame was that they met Byron, were two brothers of whom nothing else is known except that they were "both amiable, well-informed persons" and the initials of one were H.G.[2] Not the least interesting of all was a young subaltern in the Scots Greys, Thomas Gordon of Cairness, who travelled from Ioannina to Athens in 1810. Though there is no record that he ever met Byron, their lives had more in common than a common date of birth (in 1788) and perhaps even a common ancestry (for Gordon was Byron's mother's maiden name). For one thing, neither of them rushed into print with reminiscences of his travels. Both were saving themselves for greater occasions.

With so many visitors in transit or in residence, Athens was the

[1] Galt, *Voyages and Travels in the Years 1809, 1810 and 1811* (London, 1812).

[2] Anon, *A Narrative, in two parts: written in 1812* (London, 1813). The partial identification is due to a manuscript note in the copy in the Gennadius Library at Athens, but it is clear that "H—— G——" cannot be H. G. Knight, mentioned above.

scene of a gay and sophisticated society in 1810. It had not always been so, though the historic city was not the humble village it has been made out, nor were its inhabitants mere peasants. Unlike Ioannina, the cultural capital of the north, Athens had been protected from the tyranny of irresponsible Turkish governors by its status as appanage of the *kislar-aga* or chief of the Sultans' negro eunuchs—a status earned, it is said, as a reward to the beautiful Athenian slave Vasiliki, who became the mistress of an early Sultan. The city therefore enjoyed a comparative freedom from oppression. Its people were largely left to themselves, which was the happiest fate a Greek could expect under Ottoman rule. They had sufficient rudiments of education to be well aware that their history was a matter of interest to foreign visitors; and they were accustomed to the civilised society of Consuls and priests. They were ready to enjoy themselves with the foreign aristocrats, for hitherto their European visitors had not been particularly exciting.

A high-minded or utilitarian quest for knowledge had been the chief attraction to Greece for English travellers in previous centuries. There had been classical scholars galore, beginning apparently with the learned Dr. Spon and Sir George Wheler in the 17th century. There had been diplomatists from Constantinople like Sir Paul Rycaut, whose interest is shown in the title of his book: *The Present State of the Greek and Armenian Churches* (1679). Later, there had been men of science, like the botanist, Dr. Sibthorp, and the mineralogist, the Rev. E. D. Clarke, at the end of the 18th century; and these too, like all educated men of the day, were classical scholars as well. Many had left learned reminiscences: Mr. Moritt's *Account of a Journey through the District of Maina in the Morea* (1795); and Mr. Hawkins' examination in the same year of the vale of Tempe, the phenomenon of the Euripus current, and the site of Dodona. Then, as the decline of the Ottoman Empire became manifest and the rivalry over its anticipated remains became intense between France, Russia and England, the Greek lands began to swarm with military, diplomatic and even commercial agents. Colonel Leake made his first visit in 1800; a Colonel Squire, Sir John Stuart and General

Airey about the same time; naval officers were sent to survey the coast line of Aegean; and a British Consul was appointed in Ioannina. One of Elgin's agents, the Rev. Philip Hunt, also took time off from despoiling the Parthenon to visit Ioannina on a mission to Ali Pasha, who was already virtually an independent power, negotiating on his own account with European governments. At the time of Byron's visit to Ioannina, Colonel Leake himself held the post of Resident there, having extended his travels to northern Greece in 1807 and ingratiated himself with Ali Pasha. He later added *Travels in Northern Greece* (1835) to his *Travels in the Morea* (1830).

Leake's were the best, but not the earliest factual studies of Greece in English. They had a number of predecessors. Before the turn of the century, William Eton had published a *Survey of the Turkish Empire* (1798). Some thought it too pro-Russian, but very significantly it was soon translated into French. A number of collections of past writings on European Turkey were assembled for the benefit of travellers. John Pinkerton published *A General Collection of the Best and Most Interesting Voyages and Travels in all Parts of the World*, of which volume X (in 1811) included one or two accounts of Greece, but none more recent than 1745. The Rev. Robert Walpole's *Memoirs Relating to European and Asiatic Turkey and Other Countries of the East* (1818) was more up to date. It contained accounts by Dr. Sibthorp (1795), the Rev. Philip Hunt (1799), Colonel Squire, the Earl of Aberdeen, Walpole himself and others. But by common consent the most useful modern work was F. C. H. L. Pouqueville's *Voyage en Morée* in the years 1798–1801, published in 1805 and deservedly translated into English, German and Italian within a few years afterwards. The knowledge it showed of Greece and the Greeks was immense. It was also rather disturbing, for Pouqueville was Napoleon's Consul in Ioannina.

A different and more attractive quest for knowledge inspired the most interesting of Byron's predecessors in the pilgrimage to Greece. In 1788 a frail, dreamy young man of twenty-one arrived in the Ionian Islands, then still under Venetian rule. He was the Hon. Frederick North, the third son of the second Earl of Guilford, who is better known to history as George III's Prime Minister, Lord North. Frederick (later to be the fifth Earl of Guilford himself) did not visit the Greek mainland on this occasion, but he assimilated himself enthusiastically to the Greek way of life. He learned modern Greek; he gave money to a Greek school at Preveza; he wrote a Pindaric ode to Catherine II of Russia, who was then herself full of philhellenic sentiments of an imperialistic kind. Finally, in January 1791, he was received into the Greek Orthodox Church. By a lucky chance, there survives an account of his catechism and the ceremony of his baptism by a priest in Corfu; and also his declaration of religious belief, written in Italian and signed by himself on 24th January, 1791 (old style).[1] There can be no doubt of his sincerity, nor of his passionate devotion to the Greeks for the rest of his life. His family was, of course, furious, and ordered him to return at once to England, where he was recalled to his senses by being made M.P. for Banbury in 1792. To complete his rehabilitation in the way of life to which it had pleased his native aristocracy to call him, he was later sent out as Governor of Ceylon (1798–1805). But Greece had not seen the last of him.

By a curious coincidence, he was followed to Ceylon by a man whose path was to cross his own again in the Ionian Islands, more than a decade later. Sir Thomas Maitland, second son of the seventh Earl of Lauderdale, who became Commander-in-Chief in Ceylon in 1806 after years of military service in many parts of the world, could hardly have been more different from Frederick North in every respect, including his attitude towards the Greeks. When he became Lord High Commissioner of the Ionian Islands in 1815 (having previously also governed Malta for two years), he made it his duty to stamp out every spark of independence among the Greeks. Among other symptoms which he resolutely opposed was the project of Frederick North (who had succeeded as the Earl of Guilford in 1817) to found a university in Corfu. Popularly known as "King Tom", Maitland was as ferocious and dynamic as North was gentle and retiring. North's habit of parading in ancient Greek costume, even in

[1] Lavrentios S. Vrokinis: *Georgíou Prosaléndou Anékdota Kheirógrapha* (Corfu, 1879), p. 41.

the streets of London, seemed to Maitland merely ridiculous. Most people agreed with him that it showed a deplorable lack of judgement in the son of a former Prime Minister.

But North was not quite the only Englishman who found a hidden attraction in the subject Greeks. Another was Richard Church, a young soldier who first encountered the Greeks on his way to fight in the Egyptian campaign against the French in 1801. He described his early impressions to his sister from the eastern Mediterranean:[1]

"The Greeks, who are slaves to the Turks and are Christians, are as opposite a people as possible—a brave, honest, open, generous people, continually making us presents of fruit."

That first slightly superficial impression was reinforced and deepened by later experience, especially after the campaign to capture the Ionian Islands from Napoleon in 1809, when Church was Assistant Quartermaster-General of the British forces. He distinguished himself in the landings on Zante, Cephallonia, Paxos, Ithaka, and especially Santa Maura (Levkas), where he was severely wounded. Hobhouse, on tour in Greece at the same time,[2] had no more to say of the capture of Ithaka than that "the kingdom of Ulysses was surrendered into the hands of a sergeant and seven men." Wars of liberation were not much in the line of undergraduates from Cambridge; nor did Byron show any greater interest than his companion.

Church took his intrusion into Greek affairs more seriously. He was instructed, largely at his own suggestion, to raise a regiment of Greek light infantry, of which the Duke of York became honorary colonel. In this force he enlisted and trained many of the Greek irregulars known as *kléphtes* (bandits) who were later to be the heroes of the war of independence. One of the most celebrated of them, Theodore Kolokotronis wrote a letter to him with others in 1812, which showed that the confidence and affection were mutual:[3]

"Illustrious Chief,

"The experience of three years under your wise and judicious

[1] Quoted in Z. D. Ferriman, *Some English Philhellenes* p. 112.

[2] Hobhouse, vol. I, p. 4.

[3] Quoted in Z. D. Ferriman, *Some English Philhellenes*, p. 120.

leadership has more than sufficed to inform us as to your character as a zealous, benevolent, and gracious commander. At the moment of your departure we cannot help proclaiming this truth aloud, and it will be our greatest pleasure to continue to do so. We cannot do otherwise than testify publicly that you are the cause and promoter of such merits as we possess at present, and that you have nobly demonstrated the error of those European nations whose rooted prejudices will not allow them to believe that modern Greeks are amenable to discipline and instruction. We never can sufficiently express our admiration for the kind and winning manner in which you have led the Greeks to learn military science, causing them even to leave their country to enrol themselves in order to aid in this good work. In offering you, most beloved and benevolent commander, the tribute of our sincere affection and gratitude for these extraordinary benefits, we entreat you earnestly to make known our grateful feelings in quarters where they ought to be known, and to accept the unfaltering obedience and devotion of us soldiers, together with the high consideration and esteem of the other friends, undersigned, who join us in our ardent desire to welcome you back ere long.

"We have the honour to salute you with the deepest respect."

Fifteen years later, Church was to join them again in Greece as their Commander-in-Chief. On his own testimony,[1] the guiding motive of his military career in the intervening years was "to be near and in communication with Greece". To him the Greek war of independence, when it came, was literally a "holy war".

Not many Englishmen shared Church's enthusiasm, and few if any followed Frederick North's example of adopting the orthodox religion. But in less enthusiastic forms, the connection of Englishmen with Greece steadily developed. From the turn of the century, the names multiply fast, most of them of little fame or consequence. Among the few whose visits in the first decade of the new century may be counted even slightly memorable were William Gell, an archæologist and artist who was later to serve as Chamberlain to the disreputable and luckless Princess Caroline. He earned a minor

[1] Ferriman, p. 128.

immortality from Byron in *English Bards and Scotch Reviewers*, after publishing *The Topography of Troy* in 1804:

> *Of Dardan tours let dilettanti tell,*
> *I leave topography to classic Gell.*

He was luckier than some at Byron's hands: the first version of the poem called him "coxcomb Gell", but that was before the two had met. The two Scottish Earls, Elgin and Aberdeen, who were both at work among the antiquities during the same period, were more roughly handled by Byron who mocked their taste in

> *Phidian freaks,*
> *Mis-shapen monuments and maim'd antiques.*

Elgin's reputation in particular has never recovered from Byron's blistering condemnation.

The impulses are now clear which made Athens once more, on a minuscule scale, a centre of attraction to the young, the rich, the romantic, and the curious and learned travellers from the west. Two adjectives current at the time describe all or most of them. Some were philosophical; some were *dilettanti*; some—especially the aristocrats among them—were both. Those who sought knowledge, or philosophy, were scholars and archæologists and scientists like Edward Dodwell or Cockerell or Dr. Sibthorp; or the more truly philosophical in the modern sense, who sought religious truth, like Frederick North. The *dilettanti* had as their aim to improve the public taste. As early as 1762, the Society of Dilettanti in London had begun to publish a set of drawings called *The Antiquities of Athens* by James Stuart, with this end in view. It was the primary motive of the Earl of Elgin when he tried to recruit his team of artists before leaving London for Constantinople in 1798. But whatever their interests, the one thing they emphatically were not was philhellenes.

They all knew just what they expected to find in Greece, and they duly found it. The one thing their expectation did not include was the modern people of Greece. Hobhouse's account of his reactions to the first sight of Athens in 1809 may be taken as typical[1]

[1] Hobhouse, vol. I, p. 290.

"Were there no other vestiges of the ancient world than those to be seen at this day at Athens, there would still be sufficient cause left to justify the common admiration entertained for the genius of the Greeks. If the contemplation of the productions of antiquity such as they are seen in the galleries of princes, or the cabinets of the curious, affords so pure a delight, how much more gratifying must it be to behold the stupendous monuments of the magnificence of Phidias, still standing on the very spots to which, by the united taste of the statesman and the artist, they were originally assigned. These noble masterpieces still retain their grandeur and their grace, and towering from amidst their own ruins, and the miserable mansions of barbarians, present a grand, but melancholy spectacle, where you behold not only the final effects, but the successive progress of devastation, and, at one rapid glance, peruse the history of a thousand ages."

The same highfalutin' prose could be quoted from a dozen other travellers, most of them leaving the impression that they could have written it in their undergraduate essays without ever seeing Greece at all.

Not all of them, it needs to be mentioned, were British. There were Frenchmen too, of whom the most celebrated tourist was the Vicomte de Châteaubriand, later Ambassador in London, who arrived in 1806. There were Germans and Italians, whose motives in Greece were chiefly romantic and disinterested; and Russians, whose motives were certainly no more, and probably much less, disinterested than those of the British and French. And there were Americans, who were inevitably mistaken for British, especially since they often travelled with British companions. The Scottish artist, H. W. Williams, for example, was joined in Athens by Nicholas Biddle, one of the first American tourists in Greece. Another was Edward Everett, the first American to visit Ali Pasha, and later a man of pre-eminent distinction: President of Harvard University, Governor of Massachusetts, Minister Plenipotentiary in London, Secretary of State, and a legendary orator, whose finest hour came when he delivered the two-hour oration at Gettysburg which Abraham Lincoln eclipsed into oblivion in ten immortal sentences. The young

Everett carried letters of introduction to Ali Pasha from Byron; and at the court of the Pasha's son at Tyrnavo, he was honoured by a band of German musicians from Malta playing "God Save the King". Many of the newcomers from the U.S.A. were missionaries, whose philhellenism was of a condescending kind, since they despised the Orthodox religion. But none of the other nationalities adopted quite such an arrogant aloofness from the Greeks as did most of the British.

Their motives for coming to Greece were first and foremost sentimental." Nor is the expression of feelings," wrote Hobhouse,[1] "which it is the object and end of all liberal education to instill and encourage, to be derided as the unprofitable affusion of folly and affectation." So they wandered about Greece in their dream-world, oblivious of anything that had happened there since the 4th century B.C.

Dr. Henry Holland, whose interests were rather more up-to-date, observed one such tourist on the very day of his arrival in Athens, which was New Year's Day, 1813:[2]

"The English, more than any other people, have cultivated the ancient, through the modern Athens, and one of the first persons we saw in approaching the place, was an Englishman, looking over an excavation which had been made for the purposes of research."

Holland found the place full of foreign travellers and artists. Among them, he noted, were ten times as many English as French or Germans or Italians.

While the English pottered among the antiquities, the Scots were more practical. Hobhouse found a recent inscription carved on a plaster wall of the Erechtheum on the Acropolis, which read:[3] QUOD NON FECERUNT GOTI HOC FECERUNT SCOTI—"What the Goths left undone has been done by the Scots". The reference was to the removal by the Earl of Elgin of one the Caryatids, the female figures

[1] Hobhouse, vol. I, p. 215.

[2] Holland, *Travels in the Ionian Isles, Albania, Thessaly, Macedonia etc. during the Years 1812 and 1813* (London, 1815), pp. 405–8.

[3] Hobhouse, vol. I, p. 345.

which served as pillars of the porch.[1] It was only one of the controversial depredations of the Scottish Earl, who paid no more than one short visit to Athens himself. More notorious still was the removal of the sculptures from the pediments and frieze of the Parthenon, still treasured in the British Museum under the name of the Elgin Marbles. This is not the place to go into the controversy caused by Elgin's activities – a controversy which was already described as "a war more than civil" by Hobhouse in 1810.[2] It was furiously debated whether or not he should have removed the marbles; whether he saved them from destruction or did more damage than they would have suffered anyway; whether he had or had not paid for them; and even whether they were the masterpieces of Phidias or Roman copies of the time of Hadrian. Elgin suffered bitterly for his pains and was subjected to many infamous and irrelevant attacks.[3] But these are not to the present point. The point is that it never occurred to anybody, before Byron, that the removal of the Elgin Marbles might be seen as an act depriving the Greeks of their historic heritage. Nobody thought it in the least odd that the Greeks were allowed no say whatever in the matter.

Who indeed were the Greeks, and what had it got to do with them?

So wrapped up in their learned dreams were the sophisticated travellers of the early 19th century that if they noticed the inhabitants of Greece at all, it was only to amuse their intellectual fancy with classical parallels. The Hon. F. S. N. Douglas declared his purpose:[4] "to discover the countrymen of Pericles in the inhabitants of modern Athens, or to compare the sturdy mountaineer of Maina with the disciple of Lycurgus". Of course what they actually found was quite different; but it was not impossible to turn even disappointments to account. Neither the men nor the women came up

[1] A replacement was later supplied on the initiative of Frederick North, Earl of Guilford: Dodwell, pp. 353–4.

[2] Hobhouse, vol. I, p. 292.

[3] The story is well summarised by William St. Clair in *Lord Elgin and the Marbles* (Oxford, 1967).

[4] Douglas, pp. 1–2.

to expectations. But a classical survival could be satisfactorily traced here and there. Leake thought[1] the women of Mistra corresponded approximately to Homer's description of "Lacedaemon with its beautiful women." Douglas found the marriage ceremonies and dances reminiscent of the Shield of Achilles in the *Iliad*.[2] Dodwell detected classical parallels for the respectable occupation of brigandage,[3] and found ancient precedents for his observation that "the depriving people of their ears and noses, is a practice common to most parts of Turkey". Hobhouse judged the habits of life, the physical constitution and temper of the Greeks to be little changed from the ancients.[4] The same point was made by Leake, who formed the impression that the modern Arcadian shepherd had "almost reverted to the balanephagous state of his primitive ancestors".[5]

The most assiduous collector of classical parallels was a learned Anglican clergyman, the Rev. T. S. Hughes.[6] A group of boys dancing at Ioannina suggested to him some lines of Claudian. When he sat down with six other guests to dine with Ali Pasha, the number reminded him of Plato's *Symposium*. An elderly Turk at dinner put him in mind first of a character from Lucian, and then of another in Athenaeus' *Deipnosophistae*. Passages in the *Odyssey* and Xenophon's *Anabasis* flowed into his mind on the same occasion; so did another quotation from Xenophon when he thought of the women of Zalongo, who danced over a precipice rather than surrender to Ali Pasha. That seductive villain himself evoked prodigies of scholarly allusion. "His perfidy was more than Punic"; but "after having so long sustained the character of Nero, he was anxious to appear in the mask of Philopoemen". Hughes was not, of course, simply showing off. This was the style of cultivated literature in his day; and this was also the spirit in which educated men approached Greece. But

[1] Leake, *Travels in the Morea*, (London, 1830) vol. I, p. 149.

[2] Douglas, pp. 112–7.

[3] Dodwell, pp. 59, 74.

[4] Hobhouse, vol. I, p. 495.

[5] Leake, vol. I, p. 486.

[6] Hughes, *Travels in Greece and Albania* (2nd ed., London, 1830), vol. II, pp. 50–51, 58, 184, 290, 318. When in Greece, he was not yet ordained.

always there was a consistent line of thought behind it. The Greeks, if Greeks they could be called, were unworthy of their ancestors, whose true descendants were to be found in the colleges of Oxford and Cambridge. The best that Hughes' scholarship could find to say of the modern Greeks was a reference[1] to "that unfortunate race, occupants of the soil, if not the legitimate descendants of those heroes, whose names still shed a blaze of glory over the land which contains their ashes". They were unfortunately there; but they had no moral right to be.

It was in fact quite a surprise to the tourists to find Greece inhabited by Greeks at all, whom they treated with lordly condescension. A wholly characteristic exchange—characteristic indeed on both sides—was one which took place in 1805 between the erudite Edward Dodwell and the Greeks of Parga, who addressed to him an appeal for British protection against the threat of their seizure by Ali Pasha of Ioannina:[2] "We however thought proper to decline the proffered honour". Dodwell reflected a typically British aloofness, which culminated twelve years later in the actual cession of Parga to the Sultan; but what was the fate of the Greeks to the masters of the Mediterranean? In fact, they only noticed these degenerate peasants to the extent necessary to distinguish them from their heroic ancestors. The peasants themselves made the distinction easy by calling themselves *Romaioi* or Romans, as they had done since the days of the Byzantine Empire. It was a ridiculous pretension, of course; and Englishmen had a proper contempt for the Byzantine Empire, of which they had read in Gibbon or Voltaire that its history was not worthy of study. But at least the delusions of the *Romaioi* made it possible to distinguish them from the true Greeks or Hellenes. Their language was Romaic, which was quite different from the Hellenic Greek taught in the public schools and ancient universities of England. Romaic, indeed, was a "Barbarous Greek dialect".[3] When the English traveller chanced upon a Greek who presumed himself

[1] Hughes, vol. I, p. 162.

[2] Dodwell, p. 47.

[3] H. W. Williams, *Travels in Italy, Greece and the Ionian Islands* (Edinburgh, 1820), p. 164.

literate, there was always the satisfaction of convicting him of ignorance. Not a single one of them missed the opportunity.

Schoolmasters were their favourite butts. Colonel Leake, who visited a well-known school at Dhimitzána early in the century, was shocked to find the teacher persisting that his village was the site of the ancient Psophis, which the colonel was able to disprove by reference to Pausanias. But he feared that there was no hope of correcting such ignorant tradition, "which the people of Dhimitzána have been so long accustomed to, that they will probably adhere to it as long as Greece remains in its present state of darkness." Schoolmasters were indeed in Leake's view largely to blame for the low level of Greek erudition. In Tzakonia he found what seemed at first to be survivals of Doric forms of speech, but he soon concluded that they were "in many instances an effect of the imagination of *didaskaloi* or other half educated persons". Half-educated, indeed, was the most that even a schoolmaster could aspire to be.[1]

Edward Dodwell, in the same vein of learned contempt, found a schoolmaster at Mesolonghi in 1805 who was so ignorant as to pronounce the name of the poet Homer (*Omiros*) as three short syllables. All educated Englishmen knew, of course, that it was short-long-short: incredible as it might seem, the Greeks had never heard of an amphibrach. Worse was to follow. Nearby, he was shown an ancient site on which he was obliged to correct their simple errors:[2]

"The learned of Mesaloggion will have it to be Calydon; and were angry and disappointed when I proved to them that Calydon was situated several miles from this spot."

Poor simpletons! It is clear that they could not even spell the name of their own miserable village correctly. They had not got it right even when Hobhouse and Byron arrived four years later, by which time the correct spelling had become "Messalonge".[3] Since the English always knew best, with their classical education to back them, it may be added that they had other correct spellings of Mesolonghi,

[1] Leake, vol. II, pp. 60–62, 505.

[2] Dodwell, pp. 89, 99.

[3] Hobhouse, vol. I, p. 206.

too. It was Missolonghi, Mosalongi, and Missologia as well. But in any case, so barbarous a name could not have existed in the days which exercised their dreams. It was certainly unknown to the sixth forms of Westminster and Winchester; the scholars of Oxford and Cambridge could not be expected to spell or even pronounce so manifestly corrupt a solecism. Nor was it among their dreams that a dissipated poet would make the unhealthy, malodorous fishing-port outlive them all.

Hobhouse was spared an encounter with the ignorant schoolmaster at Mesolonghi, but he met a more celebrated one at Ioannina, whose family had taught there for 300 years. At first this very fact struck him as absurd, but he was disposed to add:[1]

"... before we laugh at a family of schoolmasters, we should recollect that we have in our own country an instance of the same thing, and that after all, an hereditary scholar is not a more strange being than an hereditary legislator."

That was fair enough: Byron was already a hereditary legislator and Hobhouse was to become one. But the hereditary schoolmaster, whose name was Psalida, was not let off so lightly by another learned visitor to Ioannina, the Rev. T. S. Hughes, some four years later. Hughes, who was travelling with Cockerell in 1813, found the same Psalida's presumed learning utterly ridiculous,[2] no doubt because the hereditary schoolmaster had the impudence to criticise Cockerell as "a tomb-breaker and a sacrilegious wretch". In retaliation, Hughes drew attention to three errors Psalida had made in his transcription of an epigram. His conclusion on this episode is devastating:[3]

"Nothing can show in a stronger point of view the errors into which a neglect of prosody, which they sacrifice to accent, must ever lead the modern Greeks."

No wonder it was commonly accepted among foreign travellers that there could be no question of Greek independence until they were better educated.

[1] Hobhouse, vol. I, p. 71.

[2] Hughes, *Travels in Greece and Albania* (2nd ed., London 1830), vol. I, pp. 442–3.

[3] Hughes, vol. I, p. 452.

Another traveller who suffered Psalida's pretensions to scholarship was Dr. Henry Holland, who visited Ioannina not long after the Rev. T. S. Hughes. Being a doctor, and therefore welcome to the Turks everywhere, Holland had exceptional opportunities to see everything he wanted. He was admitted, for example, to one of the Turkish palaces in Ioannina, where he found a ceiling decorated with "a sort of Eidouranion, with a tolerably exact adherence to the Copernican astronomy". He recorded many interesting observations on geology, mineralogy, on fish and birds, on earthquakes, barometric pressures, and the effects of lightning. He met, among other fellow doctors, one John Kolettis (later to be a leader of the revolution and Prime Minister of Greece), who had written "a pretty little chemical treatise in the Romaic language." But naturally, no one else had Dr. Holland's advantage of knowing Hellenic, the true Greek language.[1] He had no difficulty in exposing the ignorance of a semi-educated Greek whom he met at Kalabaka on the way from the court of Ali Pasha at Ioannina to the court of his son Veli Pasha. This young man, who was Veli Pasha's secretary, assured Dr. Holland that the monasteries known as the *Metéora* (from their appearance of "hanging in the air") were "coeval with the creation of the world". Dr. Holland "desisted from further enquiry, and commissioned him to buy eggs and milk for our supper". The smug superiority of the learned doctor wells up undiminished from his pages.[2]

Gell encountered even more shocking ignorance.[3] When he presented one of his village hosts on parting with a small globe, the foolish fellow "could not comprehend why the Americans did not slip off over the Pacific Ocean, or how the Chinese could manage to stick on at all". By contrast, all agreed that Ali Pasha, the Albanian tyrant of Ioannina was a paragon of learning compared to his Greek subjects. He could discuss America with Dr. Holland without committing any such foolish errors; not to mention European politics,

[1] Holland, *Travels in the Ionian Isles, Albania, Thessaly, Macedonia, etc., during the years 1812 and 1813* (London, 1815), pp. 133, 164.

[2] Holland, p. 232.

[3] Gell, *Narrative of a Journey in the Morea* (London, 1823), p. 360.

scientific instruments and precious minerals.[1] He asked the most intelligent questions, such as why so many milords came to Ioannina: to which the correct answer was to meet the great pasha himself. Every visitor to Ioannina was deeply impressed by his alert, virile and capacious mind. A few even noticed the bleeding heads and limbs of his subjects, with which he adorned the trees and walls along their route of entry;[2] but after all, his victims were only illiterate peasants or unfaithful mistresses. Most of them, in any case, were merely Greeks.

If there was one thing that the English traveller found more contemptible about the Greeks than their lack of scholarship, it was their degenerate religion. Frederick North was the unique exception. He had, he said in 1791, been aware for many years that his religious beliefs were at fault. On his way from Venice to Corfu, he had prayed continually before an *ikon* on the ship, and chided the Greeks aboard for failing to keep their fast. The priest who received him into the Orthodox Church found that "he loves our ecclesiastical ceremonies and is very expert in orthodox ritual". The record of their conversations amply confirms his judgement.[3] But all other visitors to Greece, particularly the Anglican clergymen, were quick to appreciate that the error lay entirely on the other side. The Rev. T. S. Hughes observed the "inane ceremonies and disgusting superstitions" and "the ridiculous and absurd mummeries of Greek worship."[4] Hobhouse doubted if "the degrading superstition of the Greek church" could deserve the title of a "Christian religion".[5] Williams found an even worse situation: "Morality and true religion reverence towards God, and love to man, seem almost unknown."[6] A gleam of light struck Dr. Holland, however.[7] It might at least be thought that the "seeming puerilities of a superstitious worship" were "well calculated to affect the feelings of the lower classes". And

[1] Holland, pp. 182–4.
[2] Holland, p. 201; Hobhouse, vol. I, p. 52.
[3] Vrokinis, pp. 11–12, 46–7, 57–8.
[4] Hughes, vol. II, pp. 81, 97.
[5] Hobhouse, vol. I, p. 146.
[6] Williams, vol. II, p. 166.
[7] Holland, p. 273.

compared to the milords on their travels, of course, all classes in Greece were lower.

Some charitably hoped to reform the Greek church. Missionaries had not yet appeared on the scene, but the Church Missionary Society was founded in 1799 and the British and Foreign Bible Society in 1804. The Church of England had hopes of succeeding where the Roman Catholics had long since failed. William Gell, however, had no doubt that the task was hopeless. His experience of Greece, which went back to 1801, led him to believe that:[1]

"All hope of reform in the practices of the Greek church is out of the question; for no Greek exists who would not rather become a Turk, than admit one improvement from any other community of Christians."

Not that this obstinacy was to their credit, for he shared the common view of Orthodoxy. In comparison with Greek paganism, he declared, Greek Christianity is a religion "which has lost all the elegance of its predecessor, without substituting a much purer faith". Even in religion it seemed, the history of the Greeks had been a steady and irreversible decline. Yet it was certainly true, as it has been since time immemorial and is still today, that the Greeks egarded Orthodoxy as a fixed, final and immutable revelation.

There might have been some hope of improvement if it were not for the priests; but the priests were indeed in a hopeless case. The inferior priests were quite uneducated, wrote Douglas:[2] "the character of their priesthood may be considered as one great obstacle to the improvement of the Greeks". As an example,[3] he quotes the case of a priest "described as conspicuous for learning" who mentioned Thermopylae as "the scene of the death of a great giant called Leonidas". That was simply not good enough for the common-room of Christ Church. Holland had an equally distressing experience. He met two priests at Delphi "who in wretchedness I could well compare with the priests of Iceland, but who entirely wanted the

[1] Gell, *Narrative of a Journey in the Morea*, p. 196.
[2] Douglas, pp. 66–8.
[3] Douglas p. 81.

knowledge which is often so remarkable in the latter".[1] As an example of their ignorance, he quotes the refusal of the Greek priests on Cephallonia to allow the potato to be planted there because they identified it with the forbidden fruit of the Garden of Eden.[2]

Such ignorance condemned them to remain poor. No doubt for the same reason, they were also venal. Travelling Englishmen were naturally bound to put the worst construction on their behaviour, as the artist, H. W. Williams, was to illustrate a few years later. A priest at Delphi was reluctant to admit him to his house because of a quarrel with a previous English traveller. Williams readily adds the explanation from his own quick insight:[3] "probably in consequence of some extravagant pecuniary demand which the latter chose to resist." Unfortunately things became no better with the passage of time. The "degraded state of religion", due to the ignorance and "infamous conduct and characters of the priesthood" were still there to be remarked[4] by James Emerson in 1825 and Aubrey de Vere in 1850. The British always found what they expected throughout the 19th century.

A few miscellaneous traits remain to be added to the portrait of the national character as revealed to the western tourists in the early 19th century.[5] The Greeks were factious. Leake found them suffering, as early as 1805 – sixteen years before the war of independence – from "the pernicious effects of the spirit of party". They were superstitious and servile to God and man. Dodwell remarked on their extreme credulity; and he observed in the manner of a Turkish governor's son with his tutor "the bloated pride of the young Turk and the humble servility of the Greek". They were unfriendly. Gell declared that "no people on earth ever equalled these peasants of Greece, in this unwelcoming species of sullen and ill-natured, as well

[1] Holland, p. 393.

[2] Holland, p. 41.

[3] Williams, *Travels in Italy, Greece and the Ionian Islands*, (Edinburgh, 1820), vol. I, p. 248.

[4] James Emerson and others, *A Picture of Greece in 1825* (London, 1826), vol. I, pp. 334–5; Aubrey de Vere, *Picturesque Sketches of Greece and Turkey* (London, 1850), p. 182.

[5] Leake, vol. I, p. 271; Dodwell, p. 153; Gell, pp. 101, 293; Hobhouse, vol. I pp.

as ineffectual spite". He found the Mainotes of the southern Pelopannese worst of all: "sunk, beyond all hope of recovery, in ignorance and prejudice". They were lazy. Hobhouse discovered that "the Greeks will do nothing without the stick". Although he admitted to finding "no very unamiable traits" in the Athenians, he noted on the same page a spirit of intrigue, mainly devoted to debating whether the French or the English should "deprive them of the last memorials of their ancient glory".

They were also liars. Leake was repeatedly disgusted by their habit of giving false information about the length of a journey.[1] He remonstrated once with the Abbot of a monastery about being misled by his brother over the distance to a certain village. "That was nothing," the Abbot replied; "he knew very well your Excellency was determined to go to that village, and he therefore told you the distance was shorter than the reality, not to alarm you." Sometimes the lies were more reprehensible: their hosts actually tried to conceal from their guests that they had food in the house. This did not stop the travellers from continuing to honour the Greeks with their presence—how else could one reveal to an appreciative public the squalor in which they lived? "The common class are filthy beyond measure," reported Williams.[2] Nor was it only the common class. Even at a priest's house, Dodwell had to put up with sleeping in the same room with the whole family, including a new-born calf.[3]

They were greedy, too. If a Greek refused to accept payment, it was because of an ulterior motive. Gell readily interpreted such a refusal to mean:[4] "We dare not say how much we wish to have." Why else should a beggarly peasant be unwilling to take money? They had no compunction, of course, about stealing from their employers: this was the common experience of every traveller. Hobhouse's dragoman "never lost an opportunity of robbing us".[5] Dr. Holland and the Rev. T. S. Hughes both had the unlucky

[1] Leake, vol. II, p. 177.
[2] Williams, vol. I, p. 210.
[3] Dodwell, p. 170.
[4] Gell, p. 369.
[5] Hobhouse, vol. I, p. 26.

experience several years apart of being robbed by the same servant, whom each of them engaged on Zante.[1] Not even independence could cure this grievous habit of cheating the milord. Twenty years later, the artist Francis Hervé reported[2] that "in most of the transactions which I had in my profession with the Greeks, they found out some means of cheating me". In this respect at least the learned tourists might have judged the Greeks to be unchanged from their classical ancestors; but for some reason they failed to appreciate it.

There were, of course, some indications that the Greeks were trying to drag themselves out of the slough of ignorance and degeneracy, even if the schoolmasters were doing little and the priests still less to help them. Douglas, the Oxford don, observed a great thirst for education:[3] "There is scarcely a paltry village without its school". But there were few books to read: those in modern Greek were mostly translations, and original works in Romaic were of little merit. (*Erotocritos*, the 17th century masterpiece of the Cretan poet, Kornaros, is dismissed by Douglas as a "vapid pastoral", but at least he acknowledged its existence.) Better still, however, there was hardly a single village where somebody could not be found who could "read and converse in the ancient Greek". Douglas thought it therefore not impossible to restore the language of classical Greece, and he was familiar with the efforts of Adamantios Koraïs and other learned men to do so. But he ended on a melancholy note:

"I fear we shall still have to regret that it is not so easy to revive the genius, the courage, and the love of freedom, as to restore the language through which these virtues were encouraged or inspired." Nor did he ever lift a finger to do so.

Dodwell, however, took a slightly more optimistic view. Education was reviving, he reported, not least thanks to the magnanimity of Douglas's cousin, Frederick North, the future Earl of Guilford.[4] Dr. Holland was also impressed by the standard of education at Ioannina, where there were no less than two Greek academies

[1] Hughes, vol. I, pp. 314–8.

[2] Hervé, *A residence in Greece & Turkey* (London, 1837), vol. I, p. 203.

[3] Douglas, pp. 73, 106.

[4] Dodwell, p. 168.

and a library. He remarked, however, the same point as Douglas:[1]

"Nearly two-thirds of the modern Greek publications are translations of European works, and whatever may be said of the powers of undirected genius, it is certainly better that for some time it should continue to be so."

The Rev. T. S. Hughes found a different way of depreciating the native Greeks. There were, it was true, two excellent Greek schools with libraries at Ioannina but they had been founded by Greeks from abroad, unable to assist Greece's "degraded sons" in any more effective way.[2] It was essential, in one way or another, not to fail to emphasise their degradation. Indeed, in recognising that there was no such thing as contemporary Greek literature, "we must reflect upon their misfortune and debasement". A literary revival was not to be excluded, but Hughes agreed with Douglas that it must be in Romaic: "if they attempt the Hellenic, they will surely fail". Only the graduates of western European universities could undertake so formidable a task as to write proper Greek.

They could extract a condescending enjoyment, of course, from the fact that the illiterate peasantry did not in the least comprehend the superior purpose of their own travels. A small boy guiding Dodwell on the road from Delphi gave him the satisfaction of letting him overhear the remark that:[3] "All the Franks are mad, but this one is the maddest of all". The sensation of being thought mad has always pleased those who know better about themselves. Leake had the same experience in the Pelopannese.[4] "Who is that infidel you have got with you? Is he a physician?" asked a peasant of his Turkish guide. "No," replied the guide in the same tone of contempt, "he is one of those milords that look for old castles." What could be more gratifying than such acute simplicity?

An even more extreme form of it was the happy experience of Gell.[5] At Mistra, a Greek eye-witness reported on his party to the

[1] Holland, p. 151.
[2] Hughes, vol. II, pp. 22, 77–9.
[3] Dodwell, p. 185.
[4] Leake, vol. II, p. 90.
[5] Gell ,p. 352.

Turkish governor that "we had been drawing the castle, measuring the country, and possessed in a box the means of transporting everything where we liked by magic, being the most dangerous persons who had ever entered the country". The Turk dismissed the story with contempt: the box, he said was a compass "which all the milords carry to show them the way". This gratifying anecdote neatly registers Gell's two main points: the Turk was less ignorant than the Greek; and he could recognise not only a compass but a gentleman when he saw one. But even the Turks, greatly as they were to be preferred to the Greeks, could amuse western travellers with their ignorance. When Hobhouse went to see the phenomenon of the tidal flow through the strait of Euboea (Negrepont)[1] the local governor was so astonished that he asked "whether I had no water of that sort in my own country?" A large crowd gathered to watch when they heard that a "Frank was going to look at the water". They were chiefly Greeks, of course, but some were Turks; and it only went to show how the ignorance and degeneracy of the Greeks could affect even their masters.

Ignorant, superstitious, factious, venal, obsequious, lazy and dirty and ungrateful: such were the universal epithets applied by the travellers from the west to the decadent peasantry who presumed to live in the lands of classical history. What exasperated the milords most about these semi-literate serfs was that they expected undying gratitude for the greatness of their ancestors; and the proofs of that gratitude were to be addressed to themselves. It was a favourite theme of Psalida, the schoolmaster of Ioannina. Dr. Holland suffered an outburst from him in 1812:[2]

"Scarcely had I been five minutes with him before he began to complain of the ingratitude of European nations, in not repaying to the Greeks of this day the benefits they had derived from their ancestors... This topic of the ingratitude of civilised Europe towards their country is a favourite one with every Greek, and they

[1] Hobhouse, vol. I, pp. 451–7.
[2] Holland, p. 162.

dwell upon it even to tediousness with every stranger who will afford his ear to them."

So the Rev. T. S. Hughes found it again a year later, when Psalida gave him the same treatment:[1]

"before the conclusion of the evening, the whole body of our nation was insulted, and accused of base ingratitude, as seeking rather to forge fresh chains for the wretched Greeks, than to break those with which they were loaded, and this in return for all the inestimable advantages we had received from the works of their ancestors."

The national grievance on this point was not extinguished even by independence. A generation later the historian George Finlay remarked of the British loan contracted in 1824, for which the lenders "never received a shilling of interest or a syllable of gratitude", that:[2]

"Indeed, the Greeks generally appear to have considered the loan as a small payment for the debt by civilised society to the country that produced Homer and Plato. The modern Greek habit of reducing everything to a pecuniary standard, made Homer, Plato & Co., creditors for a large capital and an enormous accumulation of unpaid interest."

Finlay, it should be remembered, was a staunch philhellene, even if a sardonic one. Those who did not share his sympathies expressed themselves less temperately.

These men, then, were not philhellenes. Their character emerges from their own narratives as clearly as that of the *Romaioi*. The adjectives are not their own, but they are unmistakable: complacent, priggish, humourless, smug, pedantic, insensitive, self-satisfied, bores. A typical conclusion was that of H. W. Williams, who brought back from his travels the single judgement that he was proud to be British, and the wish to erect a facsimile of the Parthenon at Edinburgh.[3] They loved the Greece of their dreams: the land,

[1] Hughes, vol. I, p. 443.

[2] Finlay, *History of Greece* (Oxford, 1877), vol. VI, p. 328.

[3] Williams, vol. I, p. 417.

the language, the antiquities, but not the people. If only, they thought, the people could be more like British scholars and gentlemen; or failing that, as too much to be hoped, if only they were more like their own ancestors; or better still, if only they were not there at all. Some treated them as if they were not there, but it was not easy to ignore them. Only when Byron arrived in 1809 did the idea first dawn, and then only slowly, that the Greeks too were people.

CHAPTER II

The Byronic Revolution

BYRON WAS UNLIKE any of the English travellers who had so far set foot in Greece. He was unlike them in being a genius, of course, but this was not yet apparent. Least of all was it apparent to his companion Hobhouse, who showed the comically insensitive side of his character when the two of them entered the Castalian cleft at Delphi to drink the water of inspiration.[1] "This was the immortal rill," he wrote in his sixth-form prose, "and we were sprinkled with the spray of the falling stream; here we should have felt the poetic inspiration . . . We drank deep of the spring, but (I can answer for myself) *without feeling sensible of any extraordinary effect.*" He could indeed speak for himself, and the italics are his own. He was doing his best certainly. "Hobhouse rhymes and journalises," wrote his companion at Delphi: "I stare and do nothing." The greatest English poet ever to taste the Castalian spring was already in the middle of the second canto of *Childe Harold.* However, he could not stand cant; he could not stand enthusiasm; and very soon he could hardly stand Hobhouse about whom he later wrote a cruel lampoon in verse, addressed to *My boy Hobby O!*

That worthy and slightly ridiculous figure always brought out the most mischievous strain of Byron's sense of humour. Destined to become Sir John Cam Hobhouse, M.P. and eventually Lord Broughton de Gyfford, always a conscientious Radical and celebrated chiefly for his one political achievement—that of inventing the phrase "His Majesty's Opposition"—he already seemed to carry an aura of impending eminence and ponderous respectability around with him on the goat-tracks of Greece. His solemnly

[1] Hobhouse, vol. I, p. 246.

sentimental approach to the classical landscape was typical of the eternal sixth-former whom his companion persistently satirised: "the European youth whom to the spot their schoolboy feelings bear," as Byron called them in a scene set near Troy in *Don Juan*.[1] Nor was Byron interested in what he called "antiquarian twaddle". "Do I look like one of those emasculated fogies?" he asked once, when invited to spend an afternoon inspecting ruins.[2] "Let's have a swim," he suggested instead. His interest was in people, not monuments; and in places only because of the people who lived in them. He was delighted to hear a boatman at Salamis talk of "our fleet" in that great battle long ago. Almost unawares, his thought comes out in the last word of a couplet from *The Siege of Corinth*:

> *Despite of every yoke she bears*
> *That land is glory's still and theirs.*

They were the Greeks; and this was almost the first personal attention that any traveller had paid to them.

There was one celebrated exception to Byron's professed lack of interest in antiquities. It forcibly confirms that personal sentiment moved him more deeply than learned curiosity. The antiquarian whom he could never forgive was the Earl of Elgin. It was not that the Elgin Marbles had a better chance of survival in Athens than in London: they had not, but that was beside the point. They belonged to the Greeks. Byron pursued Elgin's vandalism remorselessly year after year. In *Childe Harold* (1812):

> *But most the modern Pict's ignoble boast,*
> *To rive what Goth, and Turk and Time hath spared:*
> *Cold as the crags upon his native coast,*
> *His mind as barren and his heart as hard,*
> *Is he whose head conceived, whose hand prepared,*
> *Aught to displace Athena's poor remains:*

[1] Canto IV, 78.

[2] J. E. Morpurgo (ed.): *E. J. Trelawny's Recollections of the Last Days of Shelley and Byron* (London, 1952), p. 141.

Her sons too weak the sacred shrine to guard,
Yet felt some portion of their mother's pains,
And never knew till then the weight of Despot's chains.

This followed a similar attack in *The Curse of Minerva*, coupling Elgin with Alaric, who occupied but did not sack Athens at the end of the 4th century A.D. "Thy plunderer was a Scot!" he angrily reminded Minerva, repeating the denunciation of *Childe Harold*:

Blush Caledonia! such thy son could be!
England! I joy no child he was of thine.

But the truth was, in his current mood, he detested the whole British race, English and Scots alike. He was ripe for his great love affair with the Mediterranean peoples.

"I dislike England and the farther I go, the less I regret leaving it," he wrote[1] from Patras in November 1809. As a matter of fact he disliked Scotland even more—particularly his mother and the *Edinburgh Review* and later also Lord Elgin; but England stood for both his ancestral lands. Greece increasingly captivated him in his sulky mood. There were adventures to be enjoyed, like being shipwrecked on the coast of Epirus or swimming the Hellespont from Sestos to Abydos. He enjoyed even the discomforts, which so exasperated his manservant, William Fletcher, that in the end he had to be sent home in order to be rid of what Byron called

"his perpetual lamentations after beer and beef, the stupid bigoted contempt for everything foreign, the insurmountable incapacity for acquiring even a few words of any language, the plague of speaking for him, the comforts he required (more than myself by far), the pilaffs which he could not eat, the wines which he could not drink, the beds where he could not sleep, the long list of calamities such as stumbling horses, and want of tea . . ."

There, in reverse, are all the things that Byron found so agreeably different from England. But there were also the people, whom most of his contemporaries found so unattractive. Byron did not. "I

[1] Byron, *Letters and Journals*, vol. VI, p. 448.

found the Greeks polite and hospitable," he wrote.[1] Some he found even more than that. He fell in love, and brought immortality to Theodora Makri, the Consul's daughter, the Maid of Athens.

Byron also differed from his learned contemporaries about the culture of the Greeks. "I am now going to Athens," he wrote[2] from Patras in November 1809, "to study the modern Greek, which differs from the ancient." He learned it conscientiously, and several translations were included among the collection of poems he brought back from Greece. Nor did he share the conventional view that the Greeks' speech was debased, their literature non-existent, their children illiterate and their schoolmasters hardly less so. He wrote in 1811 that[3] "it is impossible to discover any nation with so great a proportion of books and their authors as the Greeks of the present century". He drew up for his own instruction a list of fifty-five modern Greek authors. It was naturally the anonymous folk-poetry, however, that appealed to him most. One of his translations was of a Greek love-song addressed to a girl called Haidée, who reappears in a more celebrated role in *Don Juan*. Another was Rhigas Pheraios' war-song: *Sons of the Greeks arise*! The two poems symbolise the twin roots of his interest in Greece; but there is no doubt which of the two inspired him more immediately in his twenty-third year. The Maid of Athens, Theodora Makri, may not have been his first or only mistress in Greek, for Byron was a fast learner.

But he had not come to Greece on a sentimental quest for the Greeks, any more than for any of the more conventional purposes of the English tourist. More than anything he wanted to get away from people, particularly the English, and even more particularly the Scots. Being half a Scot himself, detesting his mother, and having miserable memories of his childhood at Aberdeen, he extended his hatred to the whole nation. The venomous criticism of *Hours of Idleness*, his first book of poems, which appeared in the *Edinburgh*

[1] *Letters and Journals*, vol. VI, p. 444.
[2] *Letters and Journals*, vol. VI, p. 445.
[3] Z. D. Ferriman: *Some English Philhellenes*, pp. 186–7.

Review, added fuel to the flames. *English Bards and Scotch Reviewers*, flung over his shoulder at his critics as he left England in 1809, was an inadequate retort, because he could not identify his assailant (who was probably Henry Brougham). The Earl of Elgin was to provide a more satisfying target, but that lay in the future. On his way to Greece, he filled the first Cantos of *Childe Harold* with his pleasure in the company of anyone who was not a British humbug, and more especially with the charms of nature and solitude. Then came his discovery of the people of Greece: Ali Pasha (who despite his unexampled atrocities was paradoxically admired by the Greeks), the monks of Zitsa, the Greeks of Suli and Parga, the "hereditary bondsmen" to whom he now for the first time addressed his message:[1]

> *. . . know ye not*
> *Who would be free themselves must strike the blow?*

The subjection of Greece to foreign rulers deeply moved him. "Greece is no lightsome land of social mirth", he found, but it did not prevent him from enjoying himself. He enjoyed hilarious parties, which even Hobhouse's dignified prose could not completely sober down, with aristocratic young Greeks like Andreas Londos,[2] a future hero of the revolution. The grave historian, George Finlay, who joined Byron in his last crusade fifteen years later, described such a party in spirited terms which he had from the poet himself:[3]

"after supper, Londos, who had the face and figure of a chimpanzee, sprang upon a table, which appeared to be a relic of the Venetian domination, and whose antiquity rendered the exploit a dangerous enterprise, and commenced singing through his nose Rhiga's Hymn to Liberty. A new cadi, passing near the house, inquired the cause of the discordant hubbub. A native Mussulman replied, "It is only the young primate Londos, who is drunk, and is singing hymns to the new panagia of the Greeks, whom they call Eleftheria'."

[1] *Childe Harold*, Canto II, 76.
[2] Hobhouse, vol. I, p. 225.
[3] Finlay, *History of Greece*, vol. VI, p. 335n.

The Turk must be supposed not to have understood that the name of the new "blessed virgin" was Freedom.

Byron was at home with Londos because both were hereditary noblemen: he never forgot he was a lord, which was not less important to him than being a poet. But he was equally at home with the peasantry whom his learned contemporaries despised. Like them, he appreciated being entertained by Ali Pasha at Ioannina; but unlike them, he also appreciated the hospitality of the rude Suliotes who were Ali Pasha's life-long enemies. The brave Suliote "with his shaggy capote" fascinated Byron till the end of his life, much though he was to suffer from the Suliotes' wild unreliability. To Hobhouse they rated only a few learned notes: the capote or cloak was unique to Albania, he observed, on the authority of Spenser[1] (though it was Byron who supplied him with the quotation). Byron was more deeply impressed by their courage and hospitality[2] which *Childe Harold* experienced after being shipwrecked on "Suli's shaggy shore":

> *Such conduct bears Philanthropy's rare stamp;*
> *To rest the weary and to soothe the sad,*
> *Doth lesson happier men, and shames at least the bad.*

Byron more than repaid them in the last year of his life, but he was almost alone among Englishmen in appreciating their merits.

He was no less aware of the faults of the Greeks. "They are such damned liars," he would say, as crossly as any other English traveller. "They are perhaps the most depraved and degraded people under the sun," he later told his doctor, Julius Millingen.[3] Even when he spoke well of them, his praise was double-edged. "I like the Greeks, who are plausible rascals," he wrote in 1810, "with all the Turkish vices, without their courage." Here was the great difference between Byron and his contempories. He saw the defects of the Greeks, and loved them just the same. The English in Athens "agreed in the utter condemnation *nulla virtute redemptum* of the Greeks in general,"

[1] Hobhouse, vol. I, p. 134.
[2] *Childe Harold*, Canto II, 76–8.
[3] Millingen, *Memoirs of the Affairs of Greece* (London, 1831), p. 6.

and complained with a special bitterness of their ingratitude. "Now, in the name of Nemesis," asked Byron "for what are they to be grateful?" Yet he could be equally bitter, especially in the last year of his life when he was trying to save them from the Turks and from themselves. "At times Lord Byron would become disgusted with the Greeks, on account of their horrid cruelties, their importuning him for money, and their not fulfilling their promises," wrote one of the companions of his last days, Colonel Leicester Stanhope.[1] But he did not abandon them, as others did.

The virtue of Byron's philhellenism was that it was not blind. "All came expecting to find the Peloponnesus filled with Plutarch's men," wrote the same Colonel Stanhope, "and all returned thinking the inhabitants of Newgate more moral." Byron had already shed these illusions long before he joined the Greeks in 1824, but he did not then return home: he stayed to die with them. He did not mind what humbugs called their immorality: indeed, he made a kind of religion out of sin himself. He was "mad, bad and dangerous to know," in Lady Caroline Lamb's phrase; and he rejoiced in it. Nor, for the same reason, did he regard with conventional horror the degeneracy of the Greek religion. To Byron, all religion was cant, none more so than the Church of England; and this was not because he had not studied its doctrines, as he was later to show with surprising erudition in his discussions with a devout army doctor, James Kennedy, on Cephallonia in the last year of his life.[2] The reviews of *Childe Harold* accused him of lack of patriotism and religious unorthodoxy, which showed at least that they had got the point. In all these ways he set out to break the laws of an oppressive society. His sympathies were with those who did the same, and he recognised that their faults, if faults they were, were only to be expected in the circumstances in which fate had placed them.

Though Byron's devotion to freedom was catholic, his sense of privilege was selective. He expected to be treated as a peer even while he behaved as a revolutionary. The same combination of

[1] Quoted in Vulliamy, *Byron* (London, 1948) p. 239.

[2] James Kennedy, *Conversations on Religion with Lord Byron* (London, 1830).

attitudes was fairly common among the 19th century nobility; so much so that it can hardly be called inconsistency; but Byron was a pioneer. In the words of Bertrand Russell[1] – another aristocratic rebel, who was the first English philosopher to include Byron in a serious study of European philosophy – "it must be understood that the freedom he praised was that of a German prince or a Cherokee Chief, not the inferior sort that might conceivably be enjoyed by ordinary mortals." Nevertheless, even ordinary mortals were entitled to a great deal more freedom than they were getting, provided it did not interfere with the superior freedom of a poetic nobleman; and this applied just as much at home as abroad. Byron's desire to see the Greeks win their freedom was thus an extension of his desire to see the English achieve theirs to exactly the same degree, neither more nor less. From his own Olympian height, the rights of lesser men were, or should be, the same for all. Philhellenism was simply an element in a broad and catholic humanity which embraced the English labourer on the same level as the Greek peasant. Shelley too had the same vision, which he expressed more lucidly and forcefully than any of the contemporary Romantics in the introduction to *Hellas*, written in 1821 shortly after the outbreak of the Greek war of independence.

Shelley never set foot in Greece, and suffered from those very schoolboyish delusions about the Greeks which Byron treated with such scorn; but his words accurately represent a point of view which both poets shared:

"Should the English people ever become free, they will reflect upon the part which those who presume to represent their will have played in the great drama of the revival of liberty, with feelings which it would become them to anticipate. This is the age of the war of the oppressed against the oppressors, and every one of those ringleaders of the privileged gangs of murderers and swindlers, called Sovereigns, look to each other for aid against the common enemy, and suspend their mutual jealousies in the presence of a mightier fear. Of this holy alliance all the despots of the earth are virtual members.

[1] Russell, *A History of Western Philosophy* (London, 1946), p. 776.

But a new race has arisen through Europe, nursed in the abhorrence of the opinions which are its chains, and she will continue to produce fresh generations to accomplish that destiny which tyrants foresee and dread."

Not surprisingly, this paragraph was suppressed in the first edition of *Hellas*, thus proving his point that the English people had not yet become free. (It first appeared in print in 1892.) Byron could have subscribed to every word of it, and so could most of the philhellenes whom his example fired.

Holding such views as he did, Byron served as a bridge between the romantics with a literary and antiquarian taste for foreign causes and the social rebels who wanted a new order at home. Their ideas shared many fortuitous links, some logical, some self-contradictory. Byron himself ran the gamut of all the revolutionary ideas of the day, though he was often impatient with those who carried them to their logical conclusions. He was, for example, an extreme republican. "I hate even democratic royalty," he wrote in *Don Juan*;[1] and in *The Vision of Judgement*:

In the first year of freedom's second dawn
Died George the Third.

Naturally, Byron detested George IV even more than his father: it was not necessary to be a republican to do that. But like other radicals he combined his theoretical republicanism with some superficial inconsistencies. One was a deep sympathy for the unfortunate wife of George IV, Caroline of Brunswick-Wolfenbüttel. Another was his admiration for Napoleon, to whom he felt a sort of personal affinity which has been shrewdly recognised by the French, and less admiringly even by the English. In February 1814 he wrote:[2]

"Napoleon! – this week will decide his fate. All seem against him; but I believe and hope he will win – at least, beat back the invaders. What right have we to prescribe sovereigns to France?"

Though Napoleon lost in 1814, Byron remained loyal when he tried

[1] Canto XV, 23.
[2] Quoted in Vulliamy, *Byron*, p. 117.

Lord Byron

Jeremy Bentham

Sir Richard Church

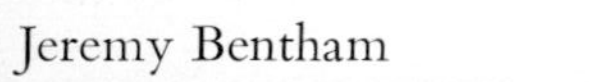

again a year later. "I'm damned sorry for it," he said of Napoleon's final defeat in "the crowning carnage, Waterloo". He never forgave Wellington his victory, which he denounced again in *The Age of Bronze* (1823) as "bloody and most bootless Waterloo".

Wellington and Castlereagh were Byron's constant butts, as they were of all radicals at the time. So too were those of his fellow-poets who had gone over to the conservative cause—Wordsworth, Coleridge, Southey—in shock at the excesses of French revolutionary imperialism. Byron stood for everything that they were against, or that he expected them in the nature of things to be against. His political friends were the radicals and the disciples of Jeremy Bentham, who were already strong in public life. He supported civil liberties, freedom of the press, Catholic emancipation; he opposed industrialisation, religious enthusiasm, the slave trade, and everything that he associated with the Establishment of the day. Only three speeches by Byron are on record in the House of Lords:[1] of these, one was in support of a Committee on the Roman Catholic claims; another was in opposition to the death penalty for frame-breaking; the third was in defence of Major John Cartwright, the "father of reform".

Frame-breaking was the offence of the so-called Luddites, who were particularly active at Nottingham, near Byron's home. He consistently defended them. "Have the military murdered any more mechanics?" he enquired in a letter from Constantinople[2] in 1810; and in 1816 he wrote a *Song for the Luddites*. But his sympathy, it is fair to point out, was expressed from a distance. He had no personal interest, one way or the other, not being an industrialist. Nor, so long as he was a land-owner, did he use his pen to attack the even greater iniquity of the Game Laws. He only denounced the "landed interest" after he had squandered his estate and ceased to share the interest.

Even in his inconsistencies, however, Byron was typical of the radical conscience of his day. There was no single, comprehensive movement for reform; there was no distinctive programme,

[1] *The Parliamentary Speeches of Lord Byron* (London, 1824).

[2] Byron, *Letters and Journals*, vol. VI, p. 452.

accepted by all its supporters and rejected by all the rest. Rather, as with the "protest movement" of the 1960s, there was a wide spectrum of progressive causes from which would-be Radicals could take their pick at will, and in some of which they would find they had Conservative allies as well. Some of the causes, though equally good in the eyes of their sponsors, led them down mutually contrary courses. Some were in the nature of things irreconcilable. Secularism and evangelicalism flourished at the same time, and both believed in religious emancipation, though for different reasons. Industrialisation provoked conflicting emotions and diametrically opposite developments. On the one hand, it increased the tyranny of capitalism and led to the sabotage of the Luddites; on the other hand, it held the ultimate prospect of a higher standard of living, and led through the foundation of Mechanics' Institutes to the improvement of education. An attempt was made to harness the industrial revolution to social welfare by Robert Owen, who published *A New View of Society* in 1813 and put his socialist theories into practice at New Lanark mill and elsewhere; but all his experiments failed, and he himself was regarded as either a dangerous or a laughable Radical. Civil liberties, freedom of the press and parliamentary reform were also double-edged weapons, especially if they passed from the hands of the privileged Radicals like Major Cartwright or Lord Byron to those of the under-privileged like Francis Place the tailor, or Thomas Hardy the shoemaker. Nationalism too was all very well on the continent: but suppose it reached Ireland?

It is not surprising that no clear and consistent pattern of adherence can be found to the progressive causes of the early 19th century. Byron espoused most of them in a haphazard way, and many of those who espoused them felt sooner or later at least an unexpressed affinity for Byron; but by no means all, nor would he have welcomed all of them to his side. The campaign against the slave-trade was a case in point. Byron was an abolitionist, of course, but so were many of his *bêtes noires*. Abolition was in fact carried in 1807 by a Tory-dominated coalition which included Byron's arch-enemy, "the intellectual eunuch, Castlereagh". It was much influenced by the high-minded Evangelical, William Wilberforce, whom Byron must have disapproved both as a Tory and as a religious enthusiast. To make matters worse, when further legislation was carried in 1810 to make participation in the slave-trade a felony, its sponsor was none other than Henry Brougham, the "Scotch reviewer" who had savaged *Hours of Idleness* a few years before. On these events Byron's voice could claim no influence, for it had scarcely yet been heard. But he would not have approved such allies. Nor would he have been best pleased to learn that after his death, when Catholic emancipation was driven through Parliament in 1829, it was achieved by his other arch-enemy, the Duke of Wellington, of all unlikely people.

Painful as it was for devoted Radicals like Byron to see their favourite causes achieved by Tories, even more exasperating were the divisions among the Radicals themselves about the causes which they ought to have supported. Exactly the same experience was repeated in the middle of the 20th century, though naturally with different content to it. In the early 19th century the contradictions were no less sincerely maintained. There were advocates of parliamentary reform who fiercely resisted Catholic emancipation and regarded the slave-trade as part of the natural order, as well as a major contribution to their income. Admirers of Napoleon changed sides as soon as they felt the breath of what was called Jacobinism on their own necks. Opponents of the slave-trade abroad voted no less conscientiously to suppress trade unions at home. So did supporters of Portuguese and Spanish nationalism vote to keep the Irish in their place. All these conflicts will be found perplexing the minds of those who were to be called philhellenes, both in London and Edinburgh and in the front line.

Byron's influence in the changing climate of opinion was not immediately obvious. In England, unlike France, Italy, Germany, and even Russia, there has been a persistent blindness to the fact that he was one of the great fertilisers of opinion in the 19th century. But in the decade which separated his first visit to Greece from the outbreak of the Greek war of independence (1811–21) it could readily have been supposed that he was simply swimming with the tide, not helping to generate it. Some faint signs of a Byronic influence began to appear among the Hellenic travellers themselves. They had read Byron from the first. Dr. Holland found Ali Pasha's court at Ioannina easy to recognise from the description in *Childe Harold*.[1] The Rev. T. S. Hughes engaged the same servant as Byron, one Dimitrios Zographos, who later distinguished himself in the war of independence.[2] He too quotes a stanza from *Childe Harold* in his account of Epirus.[3] In Athens Hughes met Theodora Makri, and noted a surprising deterioration, considering that the Maid of Athens was only three years older than when she and Byron parted:[4]

"her countenance was interesting and her eye retained much of its wonted brilliancy; but the roses had already deserted the cheek, and we observed the remains only of that loveliness which elicited such impassioned strains from the poet."

The tourists multiplied, and many of them have left behind them their informative records: John Turner, a diplomatist from Constantinople, who likewise reported on the condition of the Maid of Athens in 1812; John Bramsen and J. M. Kinneir in 1813, both of whom included Cyprus in their itinerary; a Mr. W. Jones, who visited Ali Pasha's court in 1815, and a Mr. King, chaplain to the forces in Corfu, who died at Ioannina;[5] H. W. Williams, who has already been quoted, with up-to-date information on the Maid of Athens in 1816; T. R. Jolliffe in 1817, who made the accustomed round of calls, from Ali Pasha in Ioannina to Lusieri in Athens; John Fuller and P. E. Laurent in 1818; W. R. Wilson, a fanatical Protestant, in 1819; and more than one Anon. Their tastes were similar, their prose almost indistinguishable; their works are listed in the bibliography; most of them merit no more. Few paid any more attention to the contemporary Greeks than did the pre-Byronic travellers. A partial exception must be made of the Rev. Robert Walpole, who published in 1818, as an introduction to his *Memoirs*

[1] Holland, p. 45.
[2] Hughes, vol. I, p. 323–4.
[3] Hughes, vol. II, p. 380.
[4] Hughes, vol. I, pp. 252.
[5] Hughes, vol. II, pp. 386–93.

relating to European and Asiatic Turkey, an essay on "Causes of the Weakness and Decline of the Turkish Monarchy". Here he noted the good effects of the Greeks' trading contact with Europe and the spread of education. But even he concluded that "any great national improvement is incompatible with the actual situation of the Greeks". By implication, he saw no prospect of change: still, at least he appeared to care.[1]

Byron's poetry and the romance associated with his name were not the only influence that stimulated a growing interest in Greece. Among the *dilettanti*, an even more powerful impression was made by an event which Byron himself regarded with outraged horror: the arrival in England of the Elgin Marbles, followed by their new owner's offer to sell them to the government. Ferocious debates broke out on the merits of the sculptures, the propriety of removing them from Athens, and the desirability of spending the tax-payers' money on acquiring them for the nation. The controversy culminated in 1816 in the appointment of a Select Committee of Parliament, which included F. S. N. Douglas and J. H. Fazakerly. Contemporary artists were enthusiastic about the sculptures, almost to a man: Flaxman, Nollekens, Lawrence, Turner, Wilkie, Haydon were lost in admiration; Keats and Mrs. Hemans were inspired to poetry by them; only a few academics denied their merit or their authenticity. Even Aberdeen unexpectedly praised them; but Byron was against the main stream of enlightened opinion on all counts. "Truth is," he remarked, "I am sadly deficient in gusto and have little of the antique spirit except a wish to immolate Lord Elgin to Minerva and Nemesis."

The Elgin Marbles were duly bought for the nation and helped to transform British taste, as the luckless Earl of Elgin had always hoped. Even Byron eventually admitted their merit. But in expressing his doubts, he had correctly identified the difference between his own interest in Greece and that of the *dilettanti*, who had so much of the "antique spirit" that he lacked. Inspired by the famous sculptures, they were on the move to Greece again, bent on fresh discoveries.

[1] Walpole, p. 29.

The architect Joseph Woods toured Greece between 1816 and 1818, paying much attention to the details of the monuments in Athens, and published his *Letters of an Architect from France, Italy and Greece* in 1828. Cockerell, the architect and archaelogist, continued his tireless researches till 1817. An observant and intelligent diplomatist, John Turner, explored much of Greece while serving in the Embassy at Constantinople, and made accurate descriptions of such unusual antiquities as the bridge of Arta and Nicopolis, as well as the Acropolis and of course the Maid of Athens.[1] H. W. Williams, touring Greece, in 1816 to report on "manners, scenery and the fine arts", left yet another account of Theodora Makri and her sisters.[2] Thus were ancient and modern interests reconciled under the mutually antagonistic influences of Elgin and Byron.

The main respect in which Byron left a lasting impression on later travellers is shown indirectly by the greater tolerance, sympathy and understanding with which they regarded the Greeks. Though Hughes, Holland and Williams, for example, all expressed the conventional prejudices of men like Dodwell and Gell, the aloof disdain of grandees like Elgin was mitigated by a warmer humanity. It was discovered that the Greeks were hospitable and even showed a certain self-respect. Not all of them were dirty, servile or dishonest. There was even some merit to be found in their literature. A few were more educated than had been supposed. Their religion was after all not wholly despicable. Dr. Holland reported a civilised discussion with the Archbishop of Larissa on the contrast of the Greek and Roman Catholic Churches, and a debate on the philosophy of Bishop Berkeley with a Greek doctor.[3] Hughes went so far as to attribute the degeneracy of the Greeks to their government rather than themselves. "I would make a reasonable allowance for their vices," he wrote:[4] hypocrisy, meanness and perfidy were "not inherent in their disposition". This new magnanimity again suggests the influence of Byron.

[1] John Turner, *Journal of a Tour in the Levant* (London, 1820).

[2] H. W. Williams, *Travels in Italy, Greece and the Ionian Islands* (London, 1820).

[3] Holland, pp. 367, 370.

[4] Hughes, vol. I, p. 164.

One scene in Hughes's travels is described in touching and beautiful prose of which he might fairly be judged to have been incapable before the inspiration of Byron's fresh approach to Greece and the Greeks. He had climbed Mount Mitsikeli, which overlooks Ioannina and its lake, to visit the monastery of St. George.[1] His party was met by the Abbot and some of the monks at the gates of the convent,

"which stands in a rocky recess, probably two thousand feet above the level of the lake, and immediately under the craggy summits of the mountain, where the snow lay at this time in deep ridges. The best room was allotted for our reception, and the superior did us the honour to sit at table, though his laws did not allow him to partake of our fare: he much exulted when he learned that his tutelary saint was the guardian of our native island, and assured us there was not a better or a more powerful one in the calendar. In the evening we sat in the balcony and amused ourselves in seeing the pilgrims arrive, who deposited their stores in the court-yard, and were accommodated in a long range of low rooms on the north side of the area; the apartments of the monks occupy that on the south; and between them on the eastern side stands the chapel. Fires were lighted in the court to dress the victuals, round which the different parties sat feasting, and singing to their discordant instruments: in some places various feats of strength were exhibited; in others the Romaika was danced; groups of women and children were seen scattered about the mountain, and the whole scene was full of interest and animation. Here the Greek character showed itself in its more light and airy cast, while the poor people, raised for a time above the reach of tyranny and forgetting their miseries, gave way to their feelings and indulged in all their native vivacity. At night a lovely moon, which was now in the full, shed her silvery light upon the surrounding scenery, and her rays, which were reflected in the lake below, rendered Ioannina with all the villages and hills around its plain distinctly visible. We adjourned from the convent to the edge of a noble precipice, where the mountain rises almost perpendicularly

[1] Hughes, vol. II, pp. 420–1.

from the water's edge: upon its top Antonietti had pitched our tent in the centre of a large circular threshing-floor (the *eutrókhalos aloé*) where the honest caloyers (monks) tread out their corn by means of horses and oxen. Here we sat to enjoy the luxury of a pipe and to contemplate the beautiful scene before us, whilst the night breeze threw its murmurs over the surrounding rocks, and the sounds of distant merriment in the court of the convent broke upon our ears through the general silence."

That passage is not merely moving but revealing about the young churchman-to-be. He shows himself a true disciple of Byron and the Romantic movement; but he also shows that for the first time Greece had come alive to him. So had the Greek people, and so had his own prose.

The pious hope that the Greeks might not be wholly beyond redemption particularly affected the clergy. Apart from those like Hughes, who came as classical scholars rather than missionaries, there were others who believed that the Greeks could be induced to see the light of the true or Protestant faith by a combination of preaching, education and Bible-reading. They came both from Britain and a little later from the U.S.A. At what date the Church Missionary Society, founded in London in 1799, first sent missionaries to Greece is uncertain, but it was not later than 1815. American missionaries were in Chios from 1820. The earliest dates are apparent from a publication by the Rev. William Jowett in 1822 under the title of *Christian Researches in the Mediterranean from 1815 to 1820, in furtherance of the objects of the Church Missionary Society*, the area covered including Corfu, Smyrna, Chios, Athens, Ydra and Melos, as well as Egypt. An interesting feature of this publication is its objectivity. There are comparatively few of those scornful denunciations of Greek degradation which characterised the pre-Byronic travellers. On the contrary, the book is mainly concerned with the differences of religious practice among the various faiths in the Near East—Orthodox, Copts, Jews, Moslems, Abyssinians. It is an appreciation of the problems of religious diversity rather than a summons to a Crusade. And it recognises that other nations than the British may take pride in their national diversity, expressed in religion as well as other forms of patriotism.

Patriotism was an emotion which pre-Byronic travellers in Greece had noted only for its absence. Gell in 1804 had perceived only "the improbability that any sort of public virtue should exist among the oppressed". He published his *Narrative of a Journey in the Morea* nearly twenty years later, but the lapse of time had not modified his view that independence for Greece was not to be seriously contemplated. The cause was "hopeless"; the islanders of Ydra were doomed to "extermination"; and "the little prosperity Greece was beginning to enjoy has entirely disappeared". British opinion was, he thought, deluded by the classics:[1]

"It is only from reading selections from the history of the ancient Greeks that we seem to have formed a very erroneous opinion of their political liberty . . . The country, under tyranny of the Turks, or of the Hydriotes, or the freedom of the ancient republics, is, I fear, doomed for ever to suffer under some species of *capitan pasha* or other, to the end of time . . ."

Not all readers of the classics had succumbed, however, to the delusion which Gell exposed. Douglas, the learned student of Christ Church, had not for one. He wrote no less emphatically in 1811:

"Can we believe that the effeminate prince of Fanari will join with the Mainiot in the same common cause? Will the vain Athenian submit to march in the same ranks with the rustic Moreot?"

But his question implied the same pessimism as Gell's.

The answer was that Byron had succeeded in believing these improbabilities, and his dreams were ceasing to be regarded as absurd. The notion of liberation for the Greeks was commonly accepted years before it became a reality, even if no one quite knew how it would come about. Byron's advice was no more specific than to "trust not for freedom to the Franks". Some wanted the Russians to take over Greece; others, like Douglas, thought that the Albanians would do so. But a few were converted, like Dr. Holland, to Byron's dream that "Greece might still be free", and that in the

[1] Gell, pp. vii, 219, 405, 407.

Greeks' own right. Written only a year after Douglas' sceptical conclusion, and published six years before the war of independence, the last two paragraphs of Holland's book deserve special prominence:[1]

"Of late years the Greeks, considering them in their whole extent as a people, have been making progress in population, in commerce, in education, and literature; and above all, as it would seem, in that independent consciousness of power which is necessary as a step to their future liberation. From what source this liberation is likely to arise, it would be too much to presume where the fact itself is still of doubtful occurrence. The traveller in Greece, noticing those particular vices of character which are always the consequence of slavery, and contrasting them with the temper of the ancient Greeks, might be apt to believe that their regeneration was impossible, and that political change in this country would be but the transference of submission.

"To such an opinion I cannot, from my own observation, give assent. I certainly am far from believing that the ancient Greeks, with all their peculiarities of national spirit and usage, will be revived in the people who now inhabit this country. The race has undergone many changes, – the condition of the surrounding world still more. But this belief is by no means necessary to the question; and it still remains a matter of interesting speculation, whether a nation may not be created in this part of Europe, either through its own or foreign efforts, which may be capable of bearing a part in all the affairs and events of the civilised world. Were the question proposed to me as one of probability, I should be disposed to answer in the affirmative. The further question, as to consequences, is too remote, as well as too extensive to allow me to enter into its discussion."

Hughes also, two years after Holland, recognised the rising tide of Greek patriotism in 1813. Indeed, it was almost the first thing he encountered on landing in Greece, as his diary bears witness:[2]

[1] Holland, p. 530–1.

[2] Hughes, vol. I, pp. 168–9.

"September 9th – Vain would be the attempt, if I endeavoured to express my sensations at first setting foot upon the shores of Greece; that

> *Clime of the unforgotten brave!*
> *Whose land from plain to mountain-cave,*
> *Was freedom's home, or glory's grave!*

The impression is still vivid, but it defies description. We had scarcely taken possession of the apartment prepared for us, before our host entered, leading in his hand a fine boy, about eight years of age, whom he introduced as his eldest son Themistocles: the child ran eagerly to our fire-arms, which he began to handle with delight: the father observed him with signs of pleasure, telling us that he was a brave boy, though much inferior to Leonidas his younger brother, whom he hoped to see one day heading his countrymen against their common enemy. How fiercely did vengeance, like the concealed flame of a volcano, burn in the breasts of this injured people! and how little were the Turks, sleeping in the lethargic lap of power, aware of its explosion!"

Here in the clergyman's diary can be detected a very moment of transition between two moods, both equally definite and sincere: the sentimental dream of the past combined with a passionate belief in the future, which were to characterise all philhellenic writing after Byron but were almost unknown before him. *The Giaour*, from which Hughes's quotation is taken, had been published less than four months earlier. Such was the immediacy of Byron's impact on the romantic imagination of his day.

It was not only to his English contemporaries that Byron revealed the latent force of Greek nationalism, but to the Greeks themselves as well. Hughes, who carried a copy of *Childe Harold* with him, recorded a moving episode with a Greek villager in the Peloponnese:[1]

"At one of these visits Signor Demetrio took up a copy of Childe Harold which lay upon our table, and happening to open it in the

[1] Hughes, vol. I, pp. 181–2.

appendix, that beautiful Romaic song of the unfortunate Riga beginning, *Dhéfte paídhes tón Ellínon* ("Sons of the Greeks, arise!"), met his eye: the discovery seemed to electrify him; running with the book to his companions, he communicated to them the important fact, and after a short but animated conversation, flew out of the room with the book in his hand. His friends soon followed, and as none of them returned that day, we began to fear lest these cunning Greeks might think it a good opportunity of paying their court to the pasha, and shewing their zeal, by exciting his suspicions against us and giving him some pretext for the brutality of his conduct. In that however we wronged them. The book was carried off by Demetrio, for the purpose of copying the song, and exhibiting to a few of the principal inhabitants a specimen of what was done for the Grecian cause in England: they supposed that the whole work related either directly or indirectly to the liberation of the Greeks, and the very idea created in their minds an ecstasy of joy, which it would have been a pity to damp by explanation."

Thus did Byron's poetry inspire not only susceptible English Romantics, but the Greeks themselves, less than five years after he first set foot in their country.

His influence also had another effect. He brought a new species of traveller to Greece. The scholars and the antiquarians, the artists, the diplomatists and intelligence officers, the aristocrats on the Grand Tour, continued as before, though Athens was never so glamorous a centre again as it had been in 1809-10. The travellers were venturing further afield—to the Levant, to Persia, to Arabia, to Egypt and even Ethiopia; and many of them passed Greece by altogether. But there is a special interest about two or three of those who did not. One of Byron's warm admirers was Princess Caroline, whom he also warmly championed in her morass of troubles, as did many Radicals, if only because they so detested her husband, the Prince Regent. She came to Greece in 1815, and performed the usual round of activities:[1] collecting antiquities, watching the dancing Dervishes in

[1] Louise Demont: *Journal of the Visit of Her Majesty the Queen to Tunis, Greece and Palestine,* (translated from the French, London, 1821).

the Tower of the Winds at Athens, and holding two balls for the "Grecian ladies", whose manner of dancing her lady-in-waiting found "insipid to the last degree". All this was normal form.

Princess Caroline also did something less conventional. She secured the release of several Greeks imprisoned for debt at Athens, by paying their debts for them, much to the annoyance of the Turkish governor.[1] The influence of Byron over this wild and unlucky princess is not in doubt. After her estrangement from the Prince Regent, she often entertained Byron at Blackheath, among her other supporters, including his old antagonist, Henry Brougham. She once started to write a novel set in Greece; and a copy of *Childe Harold* was specially bound for her daughter Charlotte, though it is possible that this was done by the Prince Regent rather than Caroline. At least her trip to Greece is probable evidence of Byron's influence on her wayward emotions.

Other less exalted but more useful converts followed in Byron's footsteps. One was Edward Blaquière, who came from a family of Huguenot emigrants settled in Dublin. He was by profession a sea-captain, and it was as such that he first visited the Mediterranean in 1813. As his reminiscences make clear, he did not set foot in Greece on that first journey;[2] nor did he meet Byron until 1823. But as with another buccaneering type of adventurer, E. J. Trelawny, whom Byron used as his model for *The Corsair* even before they had met, there was a natural affinity between the sea-captain and the radical poet, which made itself felt years before it bore fruit in the Greek war of independence. Obscure though Blaquière's history and motives may be, it is on record that by 1824 he was "by far the most popular foreigner in Greece", not excepting Byron.[3] This is scarcely surprising, as he found the principal characteristics of the Greeks to be industry, sobriety, abstemiousness, generosity, kindness, and devotion to their families. Most previous travellers had overlooked

[1] Demont, p. 77.

[2] E. Blaquière, *Letters from the Mediterranean, containing a civil and political account of Sicily, Tripoly, Tunis, and Malta* (London, 1813).

[3] H. Lytton Bulwer, *An Autumn in Greece* (London, 1826). p. 104.

these features, apart from Byron, and even he would not have gone so far; but it was Byron who made Blaquière a philhellene.

Another visitor to Greece whose philhellenism antedated the outbreak of the war of independence was Charles James Napier, a regular soldier with an already distinguished record, who first set foot in Greece in May 1820. Again there was an instinctive affinity between him and Byron, though they did not meet until 1823 in Cephallonia, when Napier was British Resident in the island. Napier and Byron had much in common, including an aristocratic lineage, to which both attached importance. Napier was a nephew of Fox, whose christian names he shared; and since he saw much of the great man in his youth, he was naturally a Whig in politics. But he went much further towards pure radicalism. Like many officers of his generation, he openly admired Napoleon, detested the Tory governments he served, and quarrelled defiantly with his superior officers when they failed to share his rather truculently progressive views. Thirty years later he ended by sympathising with the Chartists whom he was supposed to suppress as General Officer commanding the Northern District.

Napier's affinity with Byron can be seen not only in his affection for the Greeks—"feeling as belonging to them, I defended their cause on all occasions," he wrote a few years later[1]—but also in his admiration for Napoleon. "Millions of men sigh at his captivity and curse his gaolers," he declared;[2] and this was the more remarkable from a soldier who had been badly wounded fighting against Napoleon's armies under Sir John Moore at Corunna. At one time he nearly accepted the supreme command of the Greek forces in the war of independence. Destiny reserved him for a different glory in India. But wherever he had served, he would have deserved the judgement of his biographer (in the *Dictionary of National Biography*) that "his life was one long protest against oppression, injustice and wrong-doing". His superiors in the Ionian Islands, particularly Sir Frederick Adam (who succeeded Sir Thomas

[1] Quoted in Douglas Dakin, *British and American Philhellenes*, p. 46.
[2] Quoted in Z. D. Ferriman, *Some English Philhellenes*, p. 22n.

Maitland as Lord High Commissioner in 1824) were the indignant targets of his protests.

Of the two High Commissioners he served under, Maitland was the more remorseless in his opposition to Greek nationalism; but Napier preferred him to Adam, whom he criticised the more bitterly. Maitland was a rock, said Napier, and he showed justice and humanity even in carrying out the cession of Parga to Ali Pasha. Adam, by contrast, was like the Goodwin sands: weak, vacillating, hypocritical. He undermined the Earl of Guilford's plans for a University on Corfu, as well as the programme of road-building and other public works developed by Napier and John Pitt Kennedy on Cephallonia. Some of the chapter-headings in Napier's book, *The Colonies* (1833) are eloquent about their relationship: "How Sir Frederick Adam thinks that a gold-laced Coat and a Glass Coach are two great principles of government"; and "How my Quarrel with Sir Frederick Adam began". When Adam criticised his moustache, he cut it off and sent it to the High Commissioner in an envelope. But his antagonism was not merely personal. The root of it was Napier's belief that the Ionian Islands were not only essential to Britain's control of the Mediterranean and the route to India, but also a potential source of profit to the crown. "Should they be given up," he asked,[1] "because Sir Frederick Adam had not the talents to economise their revenues, and to draw forth their resources?" Whether his argument was right or wrong, it is an interesting proof that Napier, for all his philhellenism, did not contemplate the inclusion of the Ionian Greeks in a liberated nation-state. He was temperamentally an enlightened imperialist. His emotional attachment was sincere, but not without its inconsistencies.

Napier fully shared the faith in the Greeks' military capacity which Church had already demonstrated in practice. "A Greek is a soldier by nature," he declared.[2] Though few were so emphatic in their praise, Napier was not the only officer whose service in the Ionian Islands inspired him with an affection for the Greeks and a

[1] Napier, *The Colonies* (London, 1833), p. 17.
[2] *Ibid.*, p. 14.

devotion to their cause. Besides Church, there were also the two Kennedys, whom Byron distinguished as the Saint and the Sinner—the devout medical officer, Dr. James Kennedy, and the half-pay Captain in the Royal Engineers, John Pitt Kennedy, who was certainly no sinner. Sympathy with the Greeks touched also some of the naval officers in the Mediterranean such as Captain Rowan Hamilton, whose ship, H.M.S. *Cambrian*, was stationed in Greek waters from the early 1820s. Though he was himself a philhellene, he could be brutally frank with the Greeks, and he noted in 1827 that his officers were,[1] "almost without exception, violent anti-Greeks". Philhellenism was in fact still only the sentiment of a minority, in the eastern Mediterranean as elsewhere.

Although these philhellenes in the British armed services had nothing else in common, it is notable that all of them were dissociated by birth or descent from the mainstream of English life. Church came from a Quaker family, and was born at Cork. Though English by descent, his family looked upon themselves as Irish: when for instance, Church served under the Irish-born Count Nugent in Austria, his brother wrote[2] that "John Bull without Paddy would do badly". J. P. Kennedy, Hamilton and Napier were also born in Ireland. The names of all except Church suggest a Scottish ancestry. Again and again it will be found in the story of the philhellenes that they originated from the minority peoples of the British Isles. Even Byron was half a Scot, though he hated to admit it. It was therefore not only in their opinions that such men represented a minority. There may even have been a connection between race and ideology in the formation of this minority.

Still, it seemed likely to remain a minority. The majority of "violent anti-Greeks" certainly had powerful backing: Castlereagh and Wellington in London; Sir Thomas Maitland, the formidable High Commissioner in the Ionian Islands, together with Sir Frederick Adam, his subordinate and successor. Such men were not

[1] Quote in Crawley, *The Question of Greek Independence 1821–1833*, p. 38n.

[2] E. M. Church, *Sir Richard Church in Italy and Greece* (Edinburgh, 1895), pp. 21–2. Count (Lavall) Nugent is not to be confused with Lord Nugent, who became High Commissioner of the Ionian Islands in 1832.

Sir Francis Burdett

Lord Cochrane

Henry Lytton Bulwer

Thomas Erskine

to be converted by a poet of loose morals who had made England too hot for him. But the very existence of a minority proved that the leaven of his rebellious thought was at work; and in the end the minority was to prevail.

CHAPTER III

Philhellenism in Action

THE LONG-EXPECTED rising of the Greeks at last began in March 1821. At first it made little impression in Europe. The great powers denounced the Greeks as rebels, and then ignored them. A few romantic enthusiasts wished them well: Shelley, for instance, who wrote *Hellas* in the summer of 1821; and Major John Cartwright, now in his eighties, who wrote *Hints to the Greeks* (on the use of pikes in default of bayonets); and General Sir Richard Church,[1] who spoke of the "sublime idea" of helping to liberate the Greeks and "sighed to be with them", but could not afford the risk of resigning from the British service. There were few British volunteers in the early days, the first being Thomas Gordon of Cairness with his adjutant, Captain W. H. Humphreys, in September 1821. They were joined before the end of the year by Captain John Hane, from the Hanoverian service, but no other British names are on record in the first year, and only one of importance, Captain Frank Abney Hastings, R.N., in the second. When the gallant corps of Philhellenes was virtually annihilated at the battle of Peta in July 1822, there were no British among them: they were French, German, Swiss, Polish or Italian. In the first siege of Mesolonghi, though there were six Europeans present, none was British;[2] but "one Martin, an English artilleryman" turned up to do good service in 1823, and another was also reported there.

The most distinguished among the first philhellenes in action were Gordon and Hastings. Both were descended from aristocratic families, Gordon being from a cadet branch of one of the most famous

[1] Quoted in Dakin, *British and American Philhellenes*, pp. 26–7.

[2] Gordon, vol. I, p. 459; vol. II, p. 35; Millingen, p. 54.

clans in the history of Scotland, and Hastings a son of General Sir Charles Hastings, an illegitimate son of the Earl of Huntingdon, and a kinsman of Warren Hastings, the celebrated Governor-General of India. Both had held His Majesty's commission, Gordon in the Scots Greys, Hastings in the Royal Navy; and both had left the British service, though in very different circumstances. Gordon had resigned from the army in 1810 in order to travel, on inheriting a substantial fortune. Hastings was cashiered from the navy in 1819, after challenging his Admiral's Flag Captain to a duel for an insulting rebuke to his seamanship in the West Indies. Each of them had travelled widely after leaving the British service. Gordon became a Staff Captain in the Russian Army, where he met the Moldavian Greek brothers, Alexander and Dimitrios Ypsilantis, who were later to lead the Greek rising. Hastings settled in France to learn the language, but with no fixed object in view. These two men were both typical of that restless category of British officers who could find no adequate outlet for their energy and experience in the long peace that succeeded the defeat of Napoleon.

But they were not merely restless: they were also sincere philhellenes. Gordon became attracted to the Greeks during his Russian service; and in 1816 he married a half-Greek wife. In Hastings' case the attraction can be attributed directly to Byron. He was a great reader: on active service he was invariably equipped with a substantial library, which included Gibbon, Shakespeare and Walter Scott. In France he came across the poetry of Byron, which coalesced in his mind with the desire for action to induce him to set out for Greece. His first experience on arrival was unhappy. The Greeks took him for a spy, though they treated his American companion, George Jarvis, with profuse attention. Hastings, who was always hot-tempered and proud, reacted by addressing an angry letter to Alexander Mavrokordatos, then nominally the President of Greece.[1] After expounding his honourable intentions, his aristocratic connections, and the unjust treatment inflicted on him by his own government, he demanded the right to serve the Greeks. Matters

[1] Text in Finlay, *History of Greece*, vol. VII, pp. 343–4.

were soon put right, and his services were of great value, since he was an able officer with tactical ideas ahead of his time. No doubt the initial hostility was due to the unsympathetic neutrality shown towards the Greeks by the British administration in the Ionian Islands.

The Ionian Islands were a natural base for philhellenic activity, if there was to be any. But the High Commissioner, Sir Thomas Maitland, was determined that there should not be. He had already shown his lack of sympathy for the Greeks in 1819, when he carried out the long-delayed cession to the Turks – in effect, to the Sultan's insubordinate vassal, Ali Pasha – of the fortress of Parga. This small Greek enclave on the coast of Epirus, which had hitherto shared the sovereignty of the Ionian Islands, was now separated from them. The cession of Parga to Ali Pasha was based on an earlier treaty of doubtful validity, which the British government could safely have continued to ignore; but Maitland would not have it so. Nor would he allow more than minimal compensation to the Greeks of Parga, who abandoned their homes and retreated to Corfu rather than live under Ali Pasha. His antagonism to the Greeks was implacable. Although the islands formed a protectorate, not a colony, he behaved as High Commissioner exactly as if he were a colonial Governor, and a despotic one at that. When the revolution broke out in 1821, he even dismissed one of his staff, J. Hamilton Brown, who later distinguished himself in the war, simply for being pro-Greek. He insisted on the neutrality of the islands, and interpreted it in the most restrictive sense.

Sir Richard Church was no longer there to advocate a more generous policy. The two regiments of the Duke of York's Greek Light Infantry, which he raised and commanded, had been disbanded in 1814 under pressure from the Turkish government. After attending the Congress of Vienna as an expert adviser on the Ionian Islands, he entered the service of the King of Naples in 1815 as a Major-General, and spent several years successfully suppressing brigandage in Sicily.[1] This experience of commanding Mediterranean troops stood him in good stead in his relations with the

[1] E. M. Church, *Sir Richard Church in Italy and Greece* (Edinburgh, 1895).

Greeks, as he intended it to do; but in 1820 a revolution in Naples led to his arrest and imprisonment. He was freed in January 1821, and returned to England in retirement—knighted, but frustrated and unemployed. Others, however, were still on the spot: Frederick North (now Earl of Guilford) in Corfu and Colonel Napier in Cephallonia. But both were preoccupied with other matters: Guilford attempting to found a university, and Napier feuding with his superiors, particularly Sir Frederick Adam. Maitland and Adam, the successive High Commissioners, eventually frustrated them both.

Neither Napier nor Guilford was idle, however, in the cause of the Greeks. Napier paid four visits to Ali Pasha in Ioannina during 1820, trying to encourage him to put himself at the head of a Greek rebellion. Despite his tyrannical system of personal rule, Ali Pasha was strangely popular with the Greeks; he was also in open revolt against the Sultan; but he would not take the risk of following Napier's advice, which was in any case unauthorised by the British government. But Napier was undismayed. He continued his manœuvres in support of the Greeks, visiting Patras only a few weeks before the insurrection began. Patras was a key-point at the beginning of 1821. A Russian Consul was active there on behalf of the Greeks, and a British Consul, P. J. Green, was equally active against them. The Bishop of Patras, known as Germanos, was one of the leading conspirators, and it was he who raised the flag of revolt on 28th March, 1821. Another activist in the town was the young Makriyannis, who vividly describes the first outbreak.[1] But Napier had already gone:[2]

"To my regret I left Patras just a few days before the insurrection broke out. The Greeks may be bad. What can they be under the treatment they get? But my opinion is that they will succeed. If they do not fight hard, the Turks will chop them into *kabobs*."

Napier still did not despair of helping the Greeks. He could not agree on terms for his appointment to the post of commander-in-chief, which the Greeks offered him; but in 1826 he wrote a memorandum

[1] H. A. Lidderdale, *The Memoirs of Makriyannis*, pp. 13–15.
[2] Ferriman, p. 26.

for them outlining a plan of campaign in the Peloponnese.[1] As usual, they did not act on his advice.

Guilford meanwhile pursued a less militant line of support to the Greeks. Apart from founding his university at Corfu (which lasted only a few years, under his own presidency and chiefly at his own expense), he helped to raise money for the Greeks, and played a somewhat shadowy part in the intrigues over the choice of an eventual sovereign for Greece. A description of him during this period was recorded[2] by a philhellene who visited him a few years later in his old palace on Corfu, a maze of intricate, endless corridors, where he sat before a blazing fire surrounded by papers and books, dressed as Socrates: "his mantle pendant from his shoulder by a golden clasp, and his head bound by a fillet embroidered with the olive and owl of Athens". He was naturally a supporter of the so-called "English party", who wanted Leopold of Saxe-Coburg as sovereign (or alternatively the Duke of Sussex, a younger brother of George IV). In all this activity he was much helped by his secretary, the young Spyridon Trikoupis, who was later to become famous as a historian and a friend of Byron, over whose body he pronounced the funeral oration, in April 1824.

But what of Byron himself? He gave little sign of interest in the Greek cause at this date. He had left England for good in 1816, and settled – if that is not an inappropriate word – in Italy, where his chief interest lay in Teresa Guiccioli. Rebellion was still second nature to him, but it was the Italian rather than the Greek rebels that now attracted him. Teresa's brother, Pietro Gamba, was a member of the Carbonari, a secret society whose role in Italy was somewhat similar to that of the *Philikí Etairía* (literally, "Friendly Society") among the Greeks. Although he attended meetings of the Carbonari, it was without enthusiasm that he did so. He was feeling old at 33, and wondered in a characteristic letter[3] written in January 1821: "What is the reason that I have been, all my lifetime, more or

[1] Text in Finlay, *History of Greece*, vol. VII, pp. 340–2.

[2] James Emerson and others, *A Picture of Greece in* 1825, vol. I, p. 10.

[3] Quoted in Vulliamy, *Byron*, p. 195.

less *ennuyé?*" The cause of the Greeks had not yet come to rescue him from the sense of *ennui*, nor did it do so for another two years. Shelley, who was an enthusiast for the Greeks at a distance, had introduced Byron to his friend Alexander Mavrokordatos, a future leader of the Greek revolution, to whom he dedicated his poem *Hellas.* But Byron's mind was either on other things, or on nothing at all.

He was nevertheless inevitably a central figure in the drama that was about to unfold. His personality was the only possible link between two alliances on which British support for Greece was ultimately to depend. Otherwise quite distinct and unrelated, they were the radical reformers at home and the romantic crusaders in the field. Some of both kinds have already been introduced—all those, in fact, who were committed before 1821: Gordon, Humphreys, Hastings, Hane. But there were more, and more important ones, to come once the possibility of the Greeks' survival had become clear. A crucial date was March 1823, the month in which the British government decided to recognise Greek naval blockades. The motives for this decision, which infuriated the High Commissioner of the Ionian Islands who desired only to see the Greeks crushed, were undoubtedly the successes of the Greeks at sea. They had driven the Turkish fleet back into the Dardanelles, helped by Captain Hastings; and in December 1822 they had captured Nauplia, which was to be their capital, not without help in negotiating the Turks' surrender from Captain Hamilton, "the first public advocate of the Greek cause among Englishmen in an influential position."[1] Recognition of the Greeks as belligerents followed naturally when the news of these successes reached London.

But another event in March 1823 was perhaps in the long run of even greater importance. On 3rd March the first circular was issued of a body calling itself the London Greek Committee. The signatory was its Secretary, John Bowring, and the names of the committee were not unimpressive:[2]

[1] Finlay, vol. VI, pp. 300–1.

[2] Quoted in Gordon, *History of the Greek Revolution* (Edinburgh, 1833), vol. II, p. 84. He misspells some of the names.

The Hon. H. G. Bennet, M.P.
Jeremy Bentham
Sir F. Burdett, Bart., M.P.
Robert Campbell
Col. T. H. Davies, M.P.
Edward Ellice, M.P.
William Evans, M.P.
Lord Erskine
Lord Ebrington, M.P.
J. B. Gilchrist
T. Gordon of Cairness
J. Henry
J. C. Hobhouse, M.P.
Joseph Hume, M.P.
The Hon. C. Hely-Hutchinson, M.P.
J. G. Lambton, M.P.
T. Barrett-Lennard, M.P.
J. Maxwell, M.P.
Zachariah Macaulay
Sir James Mackintosh, M.P.
George Philips, M.P.
Lord John Russell, M.P.
William Smith, M.P.
Richard Taylor
J. Williams, M.P.

These first twenty-six members (including Bowring) had grown to eighty-five before the end of the year.[1] The additional members included the sea-captain, Edward Blaquière; Byron's old antagonist in the *Edinburgh Review*, Henry Brougham, who had made his name by the defence of Queen Caroline; the poets Thomas Campbell, Thomas Moore and Samuel Rogers; the great economist, David Ricardo; and a number of distinguished soldiers, like Leicester

[1] E. S. de Beer and Walter Seton: *Byroniana: The Archives of the London Greek Committee* (*Nineteenth Century*, vol. C, September, 1926), p. 398n. A full list will be found in Appendix II, pp. 182–4.

Stanhope and Sir Robert Wilson, together with two or three generals. There was also a number of peers and other nobility, one of whom, Lord Nugent, was later to succeed Sir Frederick Adam as High Commissioner in the Ionian Islands. There were several schoolmasters, like the celebrated Dr. John Lemprière and Dr. Samuel Parr; there were clergymen of different denominations; and there were other classical antiquarians, though of the pre-war travellers who belonged to this category, the only one who joined the Committee was H. G. Knight, now eminent as an architectural scholar. Out of nearly forty Members of Parliament, almost all were Whigs, Radicals or Independents; and most of them, in the words of the first scholars who studied the Committee's archives, were "steeped in Benthamite idealism and completely ignorant of human nature". It was a fairly typical "protest movement" of its day.

It was far from being the first philhellenic committee in Europe, or even in Britain. Isolated attempts to organise financial help for the Greeks had been made as early as 1821. The honour of starting the first subscription probably belongs to Dr. Lemprière, a Channel Islander and author of the first *Classical Dictionary* (1788), who took the initiative in the autumn of 1821. A committee to collect funds was formed in December, and the subscribers included Aberdeen, Elgin and John Russell; but the first two ventured no further, though Russell, like Lemprière, later joined the more active London Greek Committee in 1823. The purpose for which these first funds were raised was purely to finance relief for the Greeks, not to promote revolution. The same was true of a Committee formed in Edinburgh in August 1822, and of another formed by the Society of Friends, or Quakers, early in 1823. But more violent forces were already gathering to a head, and they were greatly stimulated by the Turkish massacre of the Greek inhabitants of Chios (commonly known as Scio) in April 1822. The next efforts were not to be confined to relief.

During 1822 sympathy for the Greeks, especially among journalists and other propagandists, steadily turned into anger against the Turks. Religious feeling strengthened human emotion. A series of publications stimulated these feelings, in addition to pro-Greek journals such as the *Morning Chronicle*, the *Morning Post*, the *Christian Observer* and the *Gentleman's Magazine*. Two powerful pamphlets came from the Rev. T. S. Hughes, who had been among the pre-revolutionary tourists: *An Address to the People of England in the Cause of the Greeks, Occasioned by the Late Inhuman Massacres in the Isle of Scio* (1822) and *Considerations Upon the Greek Revolution* (1823) The Rev. R. Chatfield, later a member of the London Greek Committee, followed suit with *An Appeal to the British Public in the Cause of the Persecuted Greeks* (1822) and *A Further Appeal* (1823). The Greeks thus joined the Spaniards, the Italians and the Latin Americans (but not the Irish) among the oppressed nationalities for whom British hearts should bleed and British pockets be touched.[1] The time was ripe for the London Greek Committee to go into action.

It had been anticipated already on the continent of Europe. There were philhellenic committees already formed in other capital cities, including Paris, Berne and Munich. Perhaps Madrid may claim the honour of being first in the field, but there it was thanks to the same John Bowring who took the initiative in London. It was in Madrid, too, that representatives of the Greeks, seeking a loan in western Europe, first met Edward Blaquière, who suggested that they should try the City of London. He introduced them to Bowring and others in February 1823, and so the idea of a London Greek Committee was born. The question of a loan was a separate matter, though some of the same people were involved in it, including Bowring, Ellice, and Joseph Hume. Even before the first meeting of the committee, Blaquière had set out for Greece to see how such a loan could best be used, and to make sure that the Greeks did not look elsewhere first for their money (which naturally they did). Blaquière presented an enthusiastic report to the London Committee in September 1823, but it was not spectacularly successful in raising money. The Greeks could hardly be considered a good risk. In any case, the interests of the London Greek Committee were political rather than financial, as

[1] The early initiatives are described in Virginia Penn, *Philhellenism in England* (*The Slavonic Review*, vol. XIV (1935–6), pp. 363–370 and 647–658).

was evident from the high proportion of M.P.s among its members.

The list includes a future Prime Minister (Lord John Russell) and both a past and a future Lord Chancellor (Erskine and Brougham). It also includes "Radical Jack" Lambton, the future Earl of Durham and father of independent Canada; and Alderman Sir Matthew Wood, a former Lord Mayor of London and Queen Caroline's most stalwart champion. But it includes few Tories. A Tory philhellene was still something of a contradiction in terms, not only because the fear of revolution was still strong—the tragedy of "Peterloo" lay only four years in the past—but also because the British government sought to preserve the Ottoman Empire as a safeguard against Russian expansion into the Mediterranean. There were nevertheless a few Tory sympathisers. The Rev. T. S. Hughes was one; so, probably, were other clergymen, whether or not they joined the Committee; and some of the M.P.s (such as James Scarlett) became Tories later in their careers. There were others who gave moral or financial support without joining the Committee: for instance, Dr. Martin Routh, the celebrated President of Magdalen College at Oxford, a notoriously Tory community. Two other exceptions in the Tory ranks were Sir John Gladstone, father of the Prime Minister, who gave the Committee his support in Liverpool because he believed that an independent Greece would be good for trade, and William Wilberforce, the great humanitarian, who was used to being out of step with his party.

In 1822 Wilberforce had attacked Castlereagh's hostile policy towards the Greeks in round terms:[1]

"It is a disgrace to all the Powers of Europe that, long ere now, they have not made a simultaneous effort and driven back a nation of barbarians, the inveterate enemies of Christianity and freedom, into Asia . . . I know of no case in which the power of a mighty country like England could be more nobly, more generously, or more justifiably exerted than in rescuing the Greeks from bondage and destruction."

Sentiments such as these were rare among Tories. They might be

[1] Quoted in R. Coupland, *Wilberforce* (Oxford, 1923), pp. 445–6.

shared by George Canning, who had been Foreign Secretary since Castlereagh's suicide in August 1822, but few Tories would have recognised him as one of themselves. Even Canning declared[1] of the Greeks that "there is no denying they are a most rascally set", and added that England would not dream of incurring war "for the sake of protecting Epaminondas and St. Paul." This was hardly less orthodox than the view later to be formulated by the Duke of Wellington: "Indeed there was never such a humbug as the Greek affair altogether." But unfortunately Wilberforce and his friends had something of a reputation for humbug, at least among their opponents.

Wilberforce, however, was not only a Tory but a devotee of that "vital religion" known as Evangelicalism. In particular he was the leader of the so-called "Clapham Sect", a group of high-minded philanthropists of conservative views who met at his house in Clapham. It was natural that he should carry some of his colleagues with him in his sympathies for the Greeks: among them Zachariah Macaulay, father of the more famous historian. Though Thomas Babington Macaulay was to be a celebrated Whig, his father was not. The appearance of Zachariah Macaulay's name among the London Greek Committee, though not in itself a surprise, draws attention to another feature of the list which is in a way surprising. It is the absence of a number of those names which one would expect to find most readily associated with such a cause. Several names spring to mind, linked naturally with those in the list. James Mill is absent, though intimately associated with Bentham and Ricardo. So is Zachariah Macaulay's close friend, George Grote, who had started only the year before to write his monumental *History of Greece*. It was quite another Greece that formed the subject of his history. The same was true of Sir William Gell, who took the opportunity to observe in 1823 that hitherto classical research had been more interesting than "the manners and peculiarities of the modern possessors of the Grecian soil". He noted that a change had come about, owing to "the premature attempt to establish an independent Greek

[1] H. V. Temperley, *The Foreign Policy of Canning*, p. 329.

confederacy"; but he disapproved the change, and never joined the London Greek Committee.[1]

A striking feature of the list is the number of names from what has become known in later times as the "Celtic fringe" of the United Kingdom. The Scottish and Irish poets, Campbell and Moore, may be taken as symbolic of this Celtic sympathy. The Scots predominate, as they were also to do in the fighting field. Names such as Brougham, Erskine, Gilchrist, Gordon, Hume, Maxwell, and Mackintosh, speak for themselves. Still more Scots emerged in the second wave of recruitment to the London Greek Committee: George Dundas, Sir Howard Elphinstone, Lord A. Hamilton, Douglas Kinnaird (Byron's banker), Dr. Maclean, the Rev. Dr. M'Crie. There were others too: Edward Ellice, for instance, though he came from an English family, was settled in Scotland and had part of his education at Aberdeen. It is also significant that a Greek committee had been established in Edinburgh even earlier than in London. Other names tell a similar story. The Welsh names—Davies, Evans, Williams—may be deceptive, since all of them sat for English constituences. But there were several Irishmen, all from the Protestant ascendancy. Blaquière was the son of a Huguenot settled in Dublin; James Henry was also born and educated in Dublin; Hely-Hutchinson was a member of the Irish bar, M.P. for Cork, and an implacable opponent of the union in 1800. Another representative of the "fringe" was Bowring himself, a west countryman and a Unitarian who later represented Exeter in Parliament. There is a notable correspondence to be found between the London Committee and the philhellenes in action on Greek soil so far as national origins are concerned. Perhaps philhellenism provided a kind of surrogate for nationalist emotion, which lacked expression at home.

But it must also be noted that very few of the London Greek Committee ever set foot in Greece themselves. Hobhouse, of course, had been there with Byron a dozen years before: he was always about to go out again, but never quite did so. Knight had been in Greece at the same time, but never returned. Gordon had

[1] Gell, *Narrative of a Journey in the Morea*, pp. v–vii.

taken part in the early stages of the war of independence, and was to return; Blaquière and Stanhope also went out, the former more than once; but that is all. Not one of the rest, so far as is known, ever set foot in Greece (with the exception, presumably and naturally, of three London Greeks on the Committee, one of whom was a member of the Mavrokordatos family). Nor was the reason because they were unused to foreign parts or unwilling travellers: quite the contrary. Edward Ellice had lived and worked in Canada; Lambton, of course, was also to serve there; Gilchrist and Hume had both served the East India Company as medical officers, and Mackintosh had been a judge in Bombay. Bowring was one of the most formidable globe-trotters of his generation: he was reputed to have learned fifteen languages on the spot, including Turkish, Arabic and even Chinese; but Romaic was not among them. James Henry, a well-known classical scholar, was only one degree less peripatetic than Bowring. He had wandered all over Europe on foot, and crossed the Alps seventeen times, but without ever reaching Greece. Several of the other members had seen much of Europe as officers in the Napoleonic Wars. They were not stay-at-homes, but the Greek war of independence never tempted them into the field.

Another link common to some, though a minority, of the members of the London Greek Committee was an interest in trade. The merchant adventurers of the early 19th century were an immensely influential force. They and their predecessors had developed India and the West Indies, to the material benefit of the British economy as well as their own pockets. They had shown their strength by forcing the government in 1812 to reverse the Orders in Council, which had attempted to strangle Napoleonic France by economic blockade. Their wealth and goodwill provided the material foundations of Evangelicalism and Utilitarianism alike. Hard-headed though they were, it was strangely easy to convince them that the liberation of south-east Europe would open up valuable markets for British trade. Some of the pseudo-economic experts who wrote about the Ottoman Empire at the turn of the century had encouraged this delusion. John Galt, for instance, after visiting Greece in 1809–11, published a book in 1812 "containing statistical, commercial, and miscellaneous observations" on a number of countries of the eastern Mediterranean, including Greece;[1] a year later his *Letters from the Levant* dealt not only with the "state of society, manners, opinions" in Greece, but also with that of "commerce". Napier convinced himself that the Ionian Islands could be so developed as to become more than self-supporting.[2] Henry Holland included a minute account of population statistics and sources of revenue in his description of Epirus.[3] As the Rev. Robert Walpole had observed in 1818, it was through trading contacts that western Europe first came into contact with the Greeks;[4] and it was in the interests of trade that Canning decided in 1823 to recognise Greek blockades. But the commercial prospects really lay in other parts of the eastern Mediterranean, which the Greeks, usually under foreign flags, were skilfully exploiting.

The belief that the Greek mainland and islands could be commercially exploited on a considerable scale was largely delusive. A few trading centres and their special products were exceptionally successful. Furs from Castoria, dyed yarn from Ambelakia, currants and wine from the Peloponnese; but there was not much else, apart from the smuggling of antiquities. The enthusiastic reports of amateur travellers were deceptive, but they were readily believed. Edward Blaquière, who commanded respect because he had been a merchant sea-captain, told the London Greek Committee after his first visit to Greece[5] that "the prospect of wealth and prosperity is almost boundless"; and to this absurdity he added the scarcely less exaggerated statement:

"I should have no hesitation whatever in estimating the physical strength of regenerated Greece to be fully equal to that of the whole South American continent." Blaquière perhaps deluded himself by observing the commercial successes of the Greeks in the Levant. But

[1] Galt, *Voyages and Travels in the Years 1809, 1810, 1811* (London, 1812).

[2] Napier, *The Colonies*, pp. 13–17.

[3] Holland, pp. 111–15.

[4] Walpole, p. 29.

[5] Blaquière, pp. 302–5.

these successes did not rest on the potentialities of mainland Greece, which has always been conspicuously poor by comparison with Greek colonies elsewhere. Indeed, historically, poverty has lain at the root of Greek emigration from the earliest times. Whether or not the Committee believed Blaquière's nonsense, however, there were certainly some among them who were interested in the commercial possibilities of the Greek peninsula. The elder Gladstone's interest has been mentioned. Even Byron looked upon Greece as possibly an area for speculation and emigration by the British.[1]

Such a commercial interest linked several of the leading figures. Bowring was a professional businessman during the first part of his career, though a notably unsuccessful one. Edward Ellice had served the Hudson's Bay Company in Canada—an experience which no doubt gave him ideas about the fur-trade based on Castoria (a town which takes its name from the beaver). Gilchrist and Hume had lived in a commercial atmosphere under the East India Company, even if serving in a professional capacity. The Ricardo brothers were stock-brokers, whose family firm later made a handsome profit out of the loans to the Greeks raised in the City of London. But since none of them ever set foot in Greece, it is not surprising that they allowed themselves to be completely deluded about the country's commercial possibilities. Traders who knew Greece at first hand, like the employees of the Levant Company, had no such delusions, and gave philhellenism a wide berth. A single exception may be made in favour of a young man with trading interests in the Levant, Captain Bannister,[2] who fought in Greece in 1827; but he was neither a member of the London Greek Committee nor a reliable judge of the economic prospects. Not until Nassau Senior in the 1850s did a serious British economist study Greece at first hand.[3]

Such were the prime movers in establishing the London Greek Committee: Whigs and Radicals, lawyers and parliamentarians, poets and antiquarians, merchants and reformers, Scots and Irish

[1] *Letters and Journals*, vol. VI, p. 210; Trelawny (ed. Morpurgo) p. 121.
[2] Dakin, p. 148.
[3] Nassau W. Senior, *A Journal Kept in Greece and Turkey* (London, 1859).

and other vicarious nationalists; but few philhellenes. The fact is that these men were not emotionally committed to the Greek cause, in the way that Frederick North or Richard Church were. Their motives were sincere, but quite different. They were radical reformers to whom the liberation of Greece was an incidental object. They represented a fair cross-section of an increasingly influential public opinion. They lived in what was known as the "age of improvement". Improvement could take many forms. A typical "improver" was Thomas Coke (later the first Earl of Leicester), a great agriculturist and also a Whig M.P.; and he too was a member of the London Greek Committee. Another, who also joined the Committee, was Samuel Parkes, the pioneer chemist. Philanthropy, trade and technological progress were combining to make life better for all classes at home. Eventually they must also reach "the savage tribes of America, Asia and Africa", according to an enthusiastic treatise on the steam engine.[1] What went for steam engines and agriculture and chemistry went for liberty too, and Greece was even nearer than America, Asia or Africa. So to Greece their attention was turned.

Most of the members of the London Greek Committee can be seen to be men whose motives were only indirectly philhellenic. Their primary object in life was reform, in one or all of various possible directions; and secondarily, of course, they enjoyed embarrassing the Tory government. Many of them had been doing so for years, and continued to do so for years to come. The names of Lord John Russell and "Radical Jack" Lambton, both conspicuous in the struggle for the Reform Bill a decade later, need no commentary. The same is true today of Jeremy Bentham, though at the time he was (like other prophets) less celebrated in his own country than abroad, and less influential than he was to become later, particularly after his death. The father of utilitarianism and the propagator (though not the inventor) of the slogan of "the greatest good of the greatest number" still had fewer disciples in England than in France or Latin America. They were, however, represented in force on the London

[1] Quoted in Asa Briggs, *The Age of Improvement* (3rd. impression, London, 1967), p. 24.

Greek Committee, of which he was intellectually by far the most outstanding member; and they did their best to convince him that his name had a magical influence even in Greece. The Greeks, it is true, had heard much of Rousseau and other French revolutionary writers; and they were willing to oblige anyone who wished to believe that they were deeply indebted to Bentham too.

Other members of the Committee, though little remembered in history, were eminent and influential in their day. Joseph Hume, who was credited with having added the word "retrenchment" to his party's motto of "peace and reform" had the reputation of speaking longer, oftener and worse on every kind of progressive cause than any other private member of the House of Commons. Lord Erskine had made his legal reputation by defending radicals against prosecution under the oppressive legislation which was the British government's reaction to the French Revolution. Most of the names on the list were associated with one or more of the reformist movements which were fashionable at the time: Catholic emancipation, parliamentary reform, the abolition of flogging in the army and the press-gang in the navy, suppression of the slave-trade, freedom of speech and the press, legalisation of trade unions, penal reform, and so on. Many of them also had no doubt shared other emotions in earlier years: admiration of Napoleon, for instance, and disillusionment with the Prince Regent (now King George IV), carried almost to the point of republicanism, but paradoxically expressed in passionate support for his undignified and hapless wife, Caroline of Brunswick. At the trial of the King's petition for divorce against her in 1820, the defence was brilliantly led by Henry Brougham, with the young John Williams (also on the London Greek Committee) as junior counsel.

The future Lord Chancellor had joined the Committee in the second wave. Unlike the former Lord Chancellor, Erskine, who was an original member, Brougham had no sentimental devotion to the Greek cause. Nor had he any sympathy with Byron, whose name was constantly on the lips of the Committee. It was probably Brougham who had written the vicious attack on Byron's *Hours of*

Idleness in the *Edinburgh Review*; and even if the identity of the reviewer was never positively proved, Byron had no doubt at this date who it was. Brougham's real sympathies were somewhat devious and self-interested; he enjoyed both intrigue and publicity; and his contributions to the Greek cause were characteristically opportunist. It was he, for instance, who later advised Lord Cochrane to slip unobtrusively out of the country when the Cabinet (with which Brougham was in close touch) decided in September 1826 to prevent him accepting command of the Greek navy.[1] It was also probably Brougham who leaked to *The Times* the contents of the Treaty of London in July 1827, which laid the foundations for Greek independence and precipitated the battle of Navarino. But these were indirect services to the Greeks, incidental to other purposes in Brougham's political career.

Another name among the members of the London Greek Committee stands out as a classic though perhaps extreme example of early 19th century radicalism: Sir Francis Burdett, who had first been elected to the House of Commons in 1796. The list of abuses which he attacked during his first period of election includes all those mentioned, together with a few other miscellaneous grievances as well: for example, he vehemently supported a radical agitator who was arrested for criticising the exclusion of "strangers" from the House and the secrecy of its debates. His great days came in 1807, however, when he decided to contest one of the two seats representing the constituency of Westminister. These had been traditionally divided by agreement between a Whig and a Tory, but Burdett was no respecter of conventions. Partnered by Lord Cochrane (later the tenth Earl of Dundonald) – an even more flamboyant character who was also to play a conspicuous part in the Greek affair – he won his seat in a spirited campaign, including incidentally a duel with a rival candidate, in which both were wounded.

Burdett held the seat for thirty years, but both he and Cochrane suffered for their temerity. Burdett was arrested and put in the Tower of London in 1810 for a breach of parliamentary privilege,

[1] Dakin, p. 121.

though not without a violent siege of his house in which the populace defended him and at least one soldier was killed. Cochrane's fate was even more severe: in 1814 he was charged with fraud, sentenced to a year in prison and an hour in the pillory, heavily fined, expelled from parliament, cashiered from the Royal Navy, and deprived of his knighthood. Nevertheless, this was by no means the end of Lord Cochrane, who was perhaps the most brilliant naval officer of his generation after Nelson. His reputation grew under foreign flags, particularly in the wars of independence in South America. The Greeks were later among those who called upon the abilities which his own country spurned, and Sir Francis Burdett was among those who urged him to accept their invitation. These two stormy petrels both have a place in the history of Greek independence, though both were too erratic and undependable to play the part that a more rational philhellenism would have made possible.

Another of the same kind, at least potentially, was Byron's friend Hobhouse. Though of a younger generation, he had much in common with both Burdett and Cochrane. Like Burdett, he was educated at Westminster and sat in parliament for the constituency of that name; but like Burdett too, he had pursued an erratic course in getting there, including a spell in prison for contempt of parliament. After failing to win the seat in 1819, he had published a pamphlet entitled "A Trifling Mistake", which contained a bitter attack on the political system. In it he posed the question:[1]

"What prevents the people from walking down to the House and pulling out the members by the ears, locking up their doors, and flinging the key into the Thames?"

He supplied the answer himself, that "their true practical protectors . . . are to be found at the Horse Guards and the Knightsbridge barracks". After his release from imprisonment for this gesture of contempt, he succeeded in winning the same seat in 1820. It was some time before he made a notable mark in parliament—hardly, indeed, before the struggle over the Reform Bill more than a decade later—but it was natural for him to play a leading role in the London

[1] Hobhouse, "A Trifling Mistake", (London, 1819), pp. 49–50.

Greek Committee, if only because of his known intimacy with Byron. Byron's name was kept discreetly in the background in order not to give offence to the Establishment, and particularly to the Church.

Sympathy for the Greek cause was not confined to the Committee. There were others too, who took no part in organised support, but contributed their influence as individuals. Canning and Wilberforce have already been mentioned. There were also the political journalists. Blaquière noted that in general "the conductors of the daily and periodical press", with one or two exceptions, were all sympathetic to the Greeks.[1] A conspicuous case was William Cobbett, the celebrated journalist who had alternated between attacking the Radicals and the Tories alike in his *Weekly Political Register*. One of his favourite targets was now to be the London Greek Committee's mismanagement of the loans it sought to raise for the Greeks. Another was Leigh Hunt, an embarrassing and inconstant devotee of Byron's, whose son actually volunteered to join the philhellenes but fell ill on the way to Greece. There were others who had come together to form societies for various other good causes, such as the Hampden Club (1812), which included both Lord Byron and Lord Cochrane; or the Association for the Relief of the Manufacturing and Labouring Poor (1812), which was founded by Wilberforce and also included Cochrane; or the British and Foreign School Society (1814), which propagated the educational system of the Quaker, Dr. Joseph Lancaster. Such causes may seem little connected with Greece, but charity began at home only to spread her wings abroad.

Greek independence seen from London, in fact, became just one of many interests which were sometimes thrown together in incongruous packages. Their promoters were men of strong and quarrelsome temperament who opposed each other forcibly over some causes while they reluctantly combined forces in support of others. Wilberforce and Cobbett could not stand each other; Cobbett attacked Ricardo as a "muckworm" and a converted Jew; Hobhouse

[1] Blaquière, pp. vi–vii.

detested Canning, whom he described in the House of Commons as a sophist, a rhetorician, and a political adventurer; Byron had not forgiven Brougham, and referred to Cochrane as "the stock-jobbing hoaxer". There could be no love lost between the free-thinking Benthamites and the devout Evangelicals. No extravagance of the imagination could unite all these incompatible personalities in a single army of high-minded reformers. Nor were their political alignments permanent. While Hume moved from Tory to Radical, Cobbett moved from Radical to Tory; Canning earned both a Jacobin and an anti-Jacobin label; and Sir Francis Burdett ended his days as a fox-hunting Tory squire, having run out of progressive causes to support. All of them contributed in greater or less degree to the liberation of Greece. But with very few exceptions, it was not philhellenism which inspired them to do so. It was rather a desire to use the Greek affair, along with all other suitable instruments, to embarrass the Establishment and provoke the government either to resign or to adopt more liberal policies.

It was an age of enthusiasm as well as one of improvement. The motives which led men to support the different causes of reform were diverse, sometimes incoherent, often conflicting. Some were deeply religious men, but their religions were different: there were old-fashioned Baptists, Unitarians and Presbyterians, as well as new-fangled Methodists and Evangelicals. Others were equally passionate in their hostility to all religion, whether free-thinking utilitarians like Mill and Bentham or militant atheists like Shelley and his father-in-law, William Godwin. Some accepted the industrial revolution and aimed to humanise it, like Robert Owen, by a social and educational revolution; others repudiated industrialism and defended the Luddites, like Byron. Men would come together in support of one good cause and quarrel over another. Wilberforce, for example, wanted freedom for slaves but not for organised labour; and he even opposed the educational reforms advocated by the British and Foreign School Society, because it was supported by Bentham and the non-conformists. Other Tories supported emancipation for the non-conformists but opposed it for the Roman

Catholics. When Cobbett fled to the U.S.A., he consoled himself in exile with the thought: "No Wilberforce—Think of that!—No Wilberforce!" Such were the mutual antipathies of the enthusiastic reformers.

The importance of Byron (who detested what he called "enthusy-musy") in the story of the philhellenes warrants special consideration of the position of poets and other writers in the spectrum of reform. Poets were never more politically engaged than in the early 19th century, and were not to be so again for a hundred years—perhaps not until the Spanish Civil War. Byron hated all Tories, particularly those of his comrades in the Romantic movement who had gone over to the Tories in horror of Jacobinism. Southey, Coleridge and Wordsworth had once been as rebellious as himself: he could never forgive their conversion and apostasy. He despised Wordsworth in particular, who had written in his youth of the French Revolution:

Bliss was it in that dawn to be alive,
But to be young was very heaven!

but later declared that he would retire to Austria if parliamentary reform were passed, and finally descended in his old age to writing sonnets in praise of capital punishment. Byron had flayed Wordsworth, Southey and Coleridge as early as *English Bards and Scotch Reviewers* in 1808. But he was not doctrinaire in his antagonisms. Walter Scott was another Tory, as his great compatriot Robert Burns had been before him, but Byron later became devoted to Scott, in spite of his nationality, which he shared with Byron's detested mother. "Scott, the superlative of my comparative", he called him in *Don Juan*.[1] He avidly collected the Waverley Novels as they came out. But politically the two men were far apart. Scott was bitter against the Luddites, whom Byron defended; and he was barely lukewarm towards the Greeks.

It is with Keats and Shelley that Byron shared his poetic temperament, and certainly they were at one in their emotional attachment to Greece. But the Greece to which they were each attached was

[1] Canto XV, 59.

very different, not least because Byron was the only one of the three who had ever set foot there. He looked down on Keats, partly because Keats was not a gentleman, but also because Byron was conscious of his own superior realism as a writer. He could never have written an *Ode to a Grecian Urn*: he preferred to make rhymes for a "shaggy capote". Keats's Greece was constructed partly out of reading Ovid in translation and Lemprière's Classical Dictionary; partly from English poets of the 17th and 18th centuries, who were saturated with Greek mythology at second hand; and partly out of the Elgin Marbles and Chapman's Homer, which inspired some of his finest sonnets. He did not live long enough to be inspired by the Greek revolution, which broke out a few weeks after his death. It cannot be doubted which way his emotions would have inclined him had he lived to witness it, but the Greece that inspired him was a fairy-land of mythology; and so it was too for Shelley, though with a more direct experience.

Shelley knew some of the Greeks in Italy, and he was sufficiently well-informed (or thought he was) to write in the Introduction to *Hellas* that: "The chiefs of the Greeks are almost all men of comprehension and enlightened views on religion and politics". But these were not the people he had in mind when he dreamed of Greece. The contrast between Shelley and Byron in their philhellenism is the contrast between the Greece of the *Hymn of Pan* and that of *Don Juan*. No biographical knowledge is needed to guess that Shelley never saw liquid Peneus, dark Tempe, or Pelion's shadow with his own eyes: nor would Byron, who had seen such scenes, ever have dreamed of piping over

The Sileni and Sylvans and Fauns
And the Nymphs of the woods and the waves.

Byron's own down-to-earth descriptions are those of a melancholy eye-witness:

That isle is now all desolate and bare,
Its dwellings down, its tenants passed away;

or:

> *High barrows, without marble, or a name,*
> *A vast, untilled, and mountain-skirted plain;*

or:

> *Troops of untended horses; here and there,*
> *Some little hamlets, with new names uncouth.*

Byron in fact knew Greece as it was, not as it was imagined by Theocritus and transmitted by way of Milton, Gray and Collins to his contemporaries, Keats and Shelley.

There were therefore two strands to the romantic impetus which the poets gave to philhellenism as part of the progressive movement of the day. There was the romantic realism of Byron, which appealed to men of action and their political allies; and there was the artificial romanticism of Shelley, which appealed to the aesthetes and idealists. Both could be claimed in retrospect to have served the function assigned to them in the last sentence of Shelley's *A Defence of Poetry*: "Poets are the unacknowledged legislators of the world". Byron, however, was by far the more influential in his lifetime, and much of Shelley's influence may be said to have been exercised indirectly through Byron. On almost every one of the causes of the day Byron was at one with the most progressive of the reformers, whether they were Tories, Whigs or Radicals, and whether they agreed with each other or not. So far as Greek independence was concerned, he was a natural figurehead of the movement. But the term "movement" must be qualified. There was no unity, very little organisation, and no platform common to them all. There was simply a miscellany of well-meaning individualists, many of whom adopted every new cause as it came along, with regard only to its individual merits and none to consistency, to coherence or to any comprehensive programme of reform.

A modern parallel might be with the "protest movements" of the 1960s, whose members were devoted to such causes as nuclear disarmament and the abolition of capital punishment, but might suddenly become equally impassioned about theatrical censorship or racial discrimination or the release of Greek "political prisoners". Similar motives of incoherent humanitarianism inspired the miscellaneous reformers of the first quarter of the 19th century. This is not to say that they were at heart unconcerned about the Greeks, though that is probably near to the truth among those outside the London Committee. Among the members of the Committee itself, there are many instances to the contrary, and some of them were ready, like Gordon, Stanhope and Blaquière, to go to Greece in person. Lord Erskine, in his old age, published a letter to the Prime Minister, Lord Liverpool, in support of Greek independence in 1822. A year later, he wrote an enthusiastic letter to Alexander Mavrokordatos, which was read out to the the Greek leaders at Mesolonghi on 13th December, 1823 amid great enthusiasm.[1] In it the old Lord Chancellor, who died shortly afterwards, spoke of his lifelong sympathy for the Greeks and expressed his hope that the British government would soon recognise their cause.

Bentham too was sincere in his sympathy; but it was because they were struggling to be free, not because they were Greeks, that he was sympathetic. In 1823, with characteristic enthusiasm, he engaged Dr. Samuel Parr, a celebrated schoolmaster and controversialist (often know as the "Whig Johnson"), who was also a member of the London Greek Committee, to translate into classical Greek a code which he had devised for the Greeks. But his generous sympathies were equally engaged on the side of one of the Greeks' bitterest enemies, the pasha of Egypt, Mehmet Ali, whose son Ibrahim Pasha was to be the scourge of the Peloponnese from 1825 to 1828. There was no paradox about Bentham's apparently conflicting sympathies. Mehmet Ali was also struggling to be free from his overlord, the Turkish Sultan, with whom he was later to go to war. Bentham was not therefore being inconsistent when he wrote enthusiastically to Mehmet Ali in 1828, describing him as "one of the most brilliant ornaments of the present century" at the very time when the Greeks were trying to rid the Peloponnese of the pasha's detested troops.

[1] Dakin, *British and American Philhellenes*, p. 58.

The brilliant ornament of the century was suspected (wrongly as it happened) of planning to depopulate the Peloponnese of Greeks and to replace them with Egyptian peasants, a plan of which no doubt Bentham would have disapproved. But this did not prevent him from encouraging Mehmet Ali at the same time to declare his own independence, nor from offering to educate his intended successor—perhaps none other than Ibrahim Pasha—at his own expense in England.

The lack of a whole-hearted commitment to philhellenism on the part of the London Greek Committee is also apparent in the sorry story of the British loans to the Greeks. The members of the Committee principally concerned were Hobhouse, Ellice, Burdett, Hume, Bowring and the Ricardos. None comes out of the story with much credit, and all were severely attacked at the time by Cobbett in his *Weekly Register*. Some of them certainly made personal profit out of the contracts for the loans, whereas no interest was paid to the subscribers until fifty years later, and the Greeks received very much less than the nominal value of the loans owing to the heavy rate of discount. Considering the misuse to which the loans were put, that is not in itself surprising, but it is the reputation of the philhellenes that is here at issue. George Finlay, a true if disillusioned philhellene, wrote scathingly in his old age of most of those concerned.[1] In order of guilt, he named Hume and Bowring as "deeply embedded in the financial pastry which Cobbett called the Greek pie"; Ellice and the Ricardos as profiteers from one or other of the loans; Francis Burdett as "floating on the cream of Radicalism", and Hobhouse as "supporting himself above the thin milk of Whiggery by holding vigorously at the baronet's coat-tails".

Later historians would not much amend the substance of these strictures. The best that could be said for Bowring was that he was a very unsuccessful businessman on his own account: he made no fortune for himself, and ended up as a colonial Governor in Hong Kong. Joseph Hume's apologist in the *Dictionary of National Biography* acquits him of the accusation of robbery on the feeble grounds that

[1] Finlay, vol. VI, pp. 434–5.

all he seems to have done "was to press for and obtain from the Greek deputies terms by which, on the loan going to a discount, he was relieved of his holding advantageously to himself". The Committee was not notably generous in its own financial contributions. Voluntary subscriptions that it raised, as distinct from the commercial loan, amounted to little over £11,000. The dubious reputation of many radicals in financial matters accounts for the poor response, which was noted by Byron's friend, the poet Thomas Moore, after attending a meeting of the Committee in June 1823. Their collections compared unfavourably with many other benefactors of the Greeks, such as the Society of Friends, the American philhellenic committees, and private individuals like King Ludwig I of Bavaria (whose son, Otto, became the first King of Greece) and the Swiss banker Jean Gabriel Eynard, who was the financial mainstay of the Greeks for many years.

It is not then by their personal contributions, whether financial or moral, to the Greek cause that the members of the London Greek Committee deserve to be remembered. Their claim to a place in history is as incidental as their interest in the Greek cause. What they did was to exploit a situation not of their making, which led to the departure for Greece of a number of men more worthy of admiration than the majority of their own number. These, the true philhellenes in deed and not in word alone, had for the most part very little connection with the London Greek Committee. Their order of merit is, as it happens, almost in inverse proportion to the closeness of those connections. Apart from Gordon, Stanhope and Blaquière (of whom only the first was an active combatant), few of those who went to Greece did so as a direct result of the Committee's prompting; and the few exceptions, which include Lord Cochrane, were mostly unsatisfactory in their outcome. By and large, the true philhellenes were men of another stamp.

Only one man served as a bridge between the two worlds of London and Greece: Lord Byron. To the Whigs and Radicals in London he was important because he was a lord; to the philhellenes in action, he was a practical inspiration; to the Greeks he was a poet, a hero, and a god. His contribution to the liberation of Greece is literally incomparable, unless it is to be compared with his contribution to the liberation of England. The difference is that the Greeks recognised it.

CHAPTER IV

Byron's Last Intervention

THE FIRST PHILHELLENES have already been reported in action. They were Thomas Gordon and Captain W. H. Humphreys on land in the autumn of 1821; Frank Abney Hastings and John Hane at sea in the early summer of 1822. With the latter must also be mentioned George Jarvis, the first and best American philhellene in action, who later (like Gordon) became a general in the Greek army. These, and only these, so far as is known, preceded the formation of the London Greek Committee in March 1923, though it should not be overlooked that a number of missionaries, by now chiefly American, were already in the field, working with indomitable optimism at the forlorn task of converting the Greeks to one or other of the Protestant sects.[1] With the formation of the Committee, however, new arrivals began in Greece of quite different kinds. There were the agents of the Committee, reporting on the situation or administering its funds. There were the men whose military and technical services the Committee enlisted to promote the Greek campaigns. There were also still the casual tourists, travelling in Greece as if nothing out of the ordinary were happening. There were still more of the true philhellenes, brought to the scene of action by sentiment and their own determination; and there were even some who seem to have arrived by chance, like the "English gentleman, once a midshipman in the navy", who is recorded by Finlay[2] as being "accidentally on board the Hydriot squadron as a volunteer" at the end of 1823.

[1] Stephen A. Larrabee, *Hellas Observed: The American Experience of Greece, 1775–1865* (New York, 1957), pp. 41, 52, 56.

[2] Friday, vol. VI, p. 323n.

The agents and emissaries of the London Greek Committee began descending on Greece as soon as there was any prospect of funds to support them. Nearly a year passed between the foundation of the Committee in March 1823 and the flotation of the first loan in February 1824, but that did not discourage the philhellenes from setting out in the interval. Some, being rich men like Gordon, met their own costs and contributed generously to the Greek cause from their own pocket; others were financed by the small fund of voluntary contributions collected by the Committee in advance of the loan, or simply set out on the basis of hope and credit. Blaquière was the first, even before the Committee was formed. During 1823 there followed a remarkable assortment of eccentrics, adventurers and romantics. Colonel Stanhope went out on behalf of the Committee, of which he was a member. William Parry, a clerk in the Civil Department of the Ordnance at Woolwich, was hired by the Committee as an expert in explosives, and sent out with a formidable armament of artillery and a team of nine British assistants. Two adventurous young Scots, George Finlay and J. Hamilton Brown, set out on their own under an impulse of romantic philhellenism; so did a young Irishman, James Emerson, who was later to become an eminent civil servant as Sir James Emerson Tennent. A young doctor of Dutch origin, Julius Millingen, was sent out by the Committee with medical stores. All reached Greece by the end of 1823.

They were not the only volunteers. Other more shadowy names are known: a naval deserter, William Martin, who helped to defend Mesolonghi against Turkish attack in August 1823; a Captain Henry Hesketh, who was also in Mesolonghi by November; and several others who are no more than names—Lypton, Blackett, Hyler—all assembled at Mesolonghi, before the end of the year. Parry and his team also eventually arrived there, but disappointed the high expectations placed on them. Mesolonghi had in fact become the chief rallying-point for the defence of the Greek cause. It was one of the few strongholds still in Greek hands north of the Gulf of Corinth, and it lay on the Turks' natural line of communication down the western flank of the Greek peninsula, from Albania to the Peloponnese. Mavrokordatos had rightly seen its importance, and installed himself there after quarrelling with other Greek leaders in the south. Soon it was to become even more celebrated with the arrival of new and spectacular characters on the scene. One was the Cornish buccaneer, Edward John Trelawny, in whose life-story it is literally impossible to separate truth from fiction. Another was Byron himself, who was already looked upon as the lynch-pin of Greek hopes for salvation from the west.

Legend has not exaggerated the magnitude of Byron's services to Greece, but it has obscured the hesitancy with which he assumed the mantle of heroism. It has also invested his role with a uniqueness which was less apparent at the time—a transmutation similar to that of Lawrence of Arabia a century later, with the difference that Byron made no deliberate contribution either to magnifying his own legend or to belittling the reputations of others. A natural consequence of the Anglo-Hellenic love affair of the last century and a half, interrupted though it has been by lovers' quarrels from time to time, has been the evolution of an image of Byron as the unique and sacrosanct Messiah of Greek independence, combined with the assumption that this is how it always was from the first. But in the early days Byron showed little enthusiasm for the messianic role, and other competitors might have seemed more likely to fill it. He had himself warned the Greeks to "trust not for freedom to the Franks". Yet the Frankish courts all had a watchful eye on Greece, and among the Greeks a French, a British, and a Russian party were already forming.

Of all the European governments, the British was perhaps the least likely to promote Greek independence in 1821, with the possible exceptions of the Prussian and Austrian courts. French agents, on behalf of both the Royalist and the Buonapartist causes, were active from an early date. So was Prince Ludwig of Bavaria, a fanatical philhellene, who was eventually rewarded by seeing his son Otto accepted as Greece's first king. But more important than any of these was the Tsar of Russia. The Greeks had always had a mystical feeling, based on their common Church, that salvation would come from Russia. It was strengthened when a Greek from Corfu, Count John Capo d'Istria (or Capodistrias, in Greek) entered the Tsar's service and became his joint Secretary of State from 1814. He had already struck a blow for freedom as a young man in 1807, when he led the defence of Levkas (Santa Maura) against an attack by Ali Pasha; he was a close friend of many Greek leaders, including Kolokotronis, and many philhellenes, including Guilford and Napier. But he found it too difficult to walk the tight-rope between the Greek cause and his master's attachment to the Holy Alliance – a league of autocrats for mutual defence and universal interference against liberalism, which by an unlucky chance Capodistrias himself had unavoidably helped to draft. In 1822 Capodistrias resigned, and went to live privately in Switzerland.

Many Greeks still looked to him as their saviour. They disbelieved that his severance from the Tsar was genuine. They tried to involve him in their political intrigues, not always unsuccessfully. He sent them money and advice, and pleaded their cause abroad. Eventually he became their first provisional President in 1828, and three years later he met his death at their hands. He was a tragic and admirable figure, much misjudged by British partisans. But he was not cast, by temperament or inclination, for the dramatic role that was to be played by Byron. Nor, so it seemed at the time, was Byron himself. And in Byron's case, unlike Capodistrias, there was another consideration of a discouraging kind. No one could imagine for a moment that Byron's philhellenic activities, if he brought himself to action, would be supported by even the clandestine sympathies of his government. With few exceptions (of whom the only important one, George Canning, did not become Foreign Secretary until September 1822), the leading ministers of His Majesty's Government, like all respectable people, would have regarded Byron as a disreputable outcast. It was an opinion which he himself sometimes shared in moments of depression.

For two full years he gave little attention to the Greeks or their revolution. He had lived abroad, mainly in Italy, since leaving

England for good in 1816. Poetry, his friends, dabbling in the conspiracies of the Carbonari, and his last mistress, Teresa Guiccioli, occupied part of his life; the rest was *ennui*. His correspondence shows no trace of interest in the Greeks' struggle before April 1823. Shelley's friend, Trelawny, who attached himself to Byron after Shelley's death, recorded later that he often spoke of going to Greece; but this is not dependable evidence, coming from a man who was universally regarded as incapable of telling fact from fiction. The first revival of Byron's interest in the Greeks can be dated precisely to the beginning of April 1823, and it was stimulated by the London Greek Committee. Blaquière, encouraged by Trelawny, approached him on behalf of the Committee while on his way to Greece. Byron was growing tired of Teresa Guiccioli and welcomed a distraction. He even convinced himself that he had been planning for a long time to join the Greeks, and waiting only in the hope of seeing Italy liberated first.[1] Accordingly he wrote warmly to Blaquière welcoming his proposal to call.

"I well remember," Blaquière wrote later, "with what enthusiasm he spoke of his intended visit, and how much he regretted not having joined the standard of freedom long before." Though Byron would have disliked the word "enthusiasm", his letters reflect an immediate and lively interest. But his first reaction was cautious. The proposition which Blaquière brought with him, confirmed by letters from Hobhouse and Bowring, was that Byron should go to Greece as one of three Commissioners to administer the loan which was to be raised in London. The other two Commissioners were originally to have been Napier and Leicester Stanhope, though both were later replaced. Byron questioned at first whether he was really the best man for the job, especially in view of the unpopularity of his name in England. Although he wrote to Bowring from Genoa, a week after seeing Blaquière, that "my first wish is to go up into the Levant in person", he also wrote more circumspectly to Hobhouse a few days earlier:

"I have great doubts, not of my own inclination, but from the

[1] *Letters and Journals*, vol. VI, pp. 185–6.

circumstances already stated, whether I shall be able to go up myself, as I fain would do; but Blaquière seemed to think that I might be of some use even *here*, though what he did not specify."

His uncertainty was due partly to the tenacity of Teresa Guiccioli, partly to doubts about his reputation in England and his influence with the Greeks. He talked of all sorts of alternative ways of being useful: "obtaining good information, or affording assistance"; acting as agent for forwarding "surgeon's medicines, powder, and swivels etc., of which they tell me that they are in want;" and acting as a general adviser to the London Committee. In the last capacity he sent Bowring lists of requirements in one letter after another: a park of field artillery, Italian-speaking officers ("not *raw British* soldiers") and even "a printing press and types, etc.", though this was an item he was to regret when Stanhope adopted it too enthusiastically.[1] At the same time he continued to emphasise his own wish to go in person if wanted. To Bowring, he alluded significantly to "my *not* total ignorance of Romaic". To the Earl of Blessington he wrote:[2]

"I should prefer a grey Greek stone over me to Westminster Abbey; but I would doubt if I shall have the luck to die so happily." In fact he was to have neither. The Greeks would not have denied him a stone, but the Abbey would not even commemorate his name in Poets' Corner until nearly 150 years later.

From April 1823 onwards every philhellene was drawn irresistibly to Byron, wherever he might be, and all competed for the honour of being the first to draw him into the field of action. He was accessible and helpful to all, but still irresolute. Blaquière had had to go on his way without a definite answer. Trelawny could not induce him to make up his mind. Although he chartered a ship for the journey, it seemed as far off as ever. He continued to talk of raising a foreign brigade for Greece and sending assistance of all kinds, without actually doing anything. He wrote to Hobhouse[3] introducing a young relative of Shelley's, Captain Thomas Medwin, who would "explain some plan that he has formed with regard to offering his

[1] *Letters and Journals*, vol. VI, pp. 205–11, 227–9.

[2] *Letters and Journals*, vol. VI, pp. 196, 206.

[3] *Letters and Journals*, vol. VI, p. 202.

services to the Greeks—a subject in which we are all interested". But Medwin's plans came to nothing, and it looked a time as if Byron's would go the same way. The influence of Teresa Guiccioli was still too strong for the rival attractions of heroic adventure, although her brother, Pietro Gamba, was one of those who were prepared to go with him to Greece. Even Pietro, though ready for anything, was naturally more interested in liberating his fellow-countrymen than the Greeks.

At this moment of lethargy and indecision, Trelawny set himself out to be the determining influence on Byron's life. He was a man of flamboyant energy himself, whose career was an endless succession of adventures. It began—probably, but not certainly—with his desertion from the Royal Navy some time after 1805, and ended only in 1881, when he was nearly ninety. Although he wrote two more or less autobiographical works, a good deal of his life story is uncertain. Of his two books, *Adventures of a Younger Son*, although ostensibly a work of fiction, probably contains a good deal of truth about himself. There is a marked element of sadism in it, which is presumably not fictitious; and the hatred expressed of his father, and the bullying to which he was subjected as a child and as a midshipman, may both be taken as genuine. When it was first published in 1835, the *Spectator*'s reviewer called it "the cleverest book of the season in its line—not excepting *Eugene Aram*" (which had just been published by Bulwer-Lytton). Trelawny may be counted among that interesting class of novelists who produced one novel, and that a good one. On the other hand, his ostensibly genuine reminiscences—*Recollections of the Last Days of Shelley and Byron*, published in 1858—are less dependable than he would have them appear.

Everyone who knew Trelawny well recognised him as a congenital liar. Byron, who looked down on him as a social inferior, said that "he could not tell the truth to save his life". George Finlay told Richard Monckton Milnes[1] ten years later that "Trelawny would be a good fellow if he could spell and speak the truth". Nevertheless his relationship with Shelley and Byron in the last years

[1] James Pope-Hennessy: *Monckton Milnes—the Years of Promise* (London, 1949), p. 60.

of their lives was an important fact. He had a natural attraction for the romantic poets: Byron had based characters in *The Corsair* and *Don Juan* on his reputed personality before they ever met. Physical descriptions of him by contemporaries combine to depict a tall, dark, agile figure with a flowing beard and scintillating, magnetic eyes. Mary Shelley called him "a kind of half Arab Englishman", and Fanny Kemble, the actress, spoke in similar terms of "a curious being, a savage in some respects", with a "face as dark as a Moor's". Others speak of his haughty manner and lofty language. His stories about himself included piracy in the South Seas and fighting with the Wahhabis in Arabia. Little is known for certain before he turned up in Pisa in January 1822 to seek the acquaintance of Shelley, through whom he met Byron. It was he who ordered the boat which cost Shelley his life, though he did not approve its construction and warned the poet against the fatal cruise. It was he too who took charge of the cremation of Shelley's corpse in July 1822.

Then he transferred his addiction to Byron, and pressed upon him the notion of going to Greece. Personally, he would have been just as happy to renew his piratical career anywhere in the world: he also had South America in mind, where Lord Cochrane had already made himself a great name. But the attractions of Greece were obvious. Byron told him, by his own account, that he had been happier in Greece than anywhere before or since:[1] "and if I have ever written well (as the world says I have, but which they will pardon my doubting) it was in Greece—or of Greece". If new adventures were to be sought anywhere, and if Byron was to be stirred to action at all, it would have to be in Greece. Besides, the Suliotes had a national costume which Trelawny found personally becoming; and there were characters after his own heart at large in the Greek mountains, including the celebrated *kléphtes*, Theodore Kolokotronis and Odysseus Androutsos. During the winter of 1822–23, Trelawny set about restoring Byron's will to action. After the first spasm of excitement on meeting Blaquière and receiving the London Committee's invitation it fell to

[1] Iris Origo, *The Last Attachment* (London, 1949), p. 354.

Trelawny—by his own account at least—to consolidate Byron's resolution.

His resolution returned in June, when he wrote a classic and decisive letter to Trelawny:[1]

"My dear T.,—You must have heard that I am going to Greece. Why do you not come to me? I want your aid, and am exceedingly anxious to see you. Pray come, for I am at last determined to go to Greece; it is the only place I was ever contented in. I am serious, and did not write before, as I might have given you a journey for nothing; they all say I can be of use in Greece. I do not know how, nor do they; but at all events let us go.

Yours, etc., truly,

N. Byron.

A month later he set sail from Genoa for Cephallonia, accompanied by Trelawny and Teresa's brother, Pietro Gamba, and joined on the way at Leghorn by J. Hamilton Brown, the young official whom Sir Thomas Maitland had dismissed from his service in the Ionian Islands for his pro-Greek sympathies. Byron's last letter from Leghorn, on 24th July, was addressed to Goethe, to thank him for some verses written in his own hand, and to promise that "if ever I come back, I will pay a visit to Weimar, to offer the sincere homage of one of the many millions of your admirers".[2]

He chose Cephallonia as his destination because of the known sympathies of Colonel Napier, now the British Resident in the island. Once there, it seemed as if his resolution had failed again. He settled in a cottage at the village of Metaxata, and scarcely moved for four months. During that time many philhellenes called upon him on the way to Greece, as also did representatives of the provisional Greek government. To most of them he talked in despondent terms, partly because he was in a state of chronic depression and partly because he felt he had been deceived by the London Committee, who had not yet even launched the loan on which all depended. The Greeks disappointed him, though he cannot have been

[1] *Letters and Journals*, vol. VI, p. 224.
[2] *Letters and Journals*, vol. VI, pp. 237–8.

surprised, as he found a survivor of the German philhellenes was, that "the Greeks are not quite the same with them of the time of Themistocles". He never thought of going back; but at times he seemed to have no thought of going forward either.

At first he was simply delighted to be back on Greek soil, and in sight of the Greek mainland. "I don't know how it is," he told Trelawny, "but I feel as if the eleven long years of bitterness I have passed through since I was here, were taken off my shoulders, and I was scudding through the Greek archipelago with old Bathurst in his frigate." One can understand his motives: Greece was the only spot in his life where he had suffered no disappointments and done nothing of which he was ashamed. There is a happy irony, too, in his mention of Bathurst, a gallant officer who was destined to die in action four years later in the decisive battle of Navarino, as captain of H.M.S. *Genoa* in the sixty-ninth year of his life. He would not have been ashamed of the company of Byron, as so many of his fellow-countrymen were. Nor were the officers of the garrison of Cephallonia, under the enlightened command of the philhellene Colonel Napier. Even a private soldier under his command, whose strikingly interesting letters have been preserved, was aware that the garrison was entertaining no ordinary man.[1] Byron enjoyed being a person of consequence, and for the time being the atmosphere of Cephallonia and his own mood of gratified inertia suited him well enough.

It was not that the desire for action had entirely deserted him. But it must be purposive action, not the idle amusements of a gentleman of leisure. A revealing incident occurred while he was on Cephallonia.[2] A landslip near Metaxata, where he was living, buried a number of peasants alive under a mass of earth. Byron was having dinner when the news of it reached him. At once he ran to the spot, taking his doctor with him. Other villagers, who were digging their companions out, became frightened of a further landslide and refused to go on, saying that they had already dug out all the bodies. Byron

[1] *The Letters of Private Wheeler, 1809–1828* (ed. Liddell Hart, London, 1951), p. 236.

[2] Thomas Medwin, *Journal of the Conversations of Lord Byron* (London, 1824), p. 235.

was unconvinced. He tried to persuade them to continue digging, but when they would not, he seized a spade and began digging himself. In the end the villagers followed his example, and two more victims were extricated alive. Without Byron's intervention, they would certainly not have survived. It was one of the rare moments of satisfying activity during his stay on Cephallonia, in a sense foreshadowing the larger role he was seeking to play in Greece. But still the decisive impetus eluded him. Between the spasms of energy, he relapsed into watchful inactivity.

To move him on from Cephallonia, where he was still on British territory, proved almost as difficult as to get him there from Italy. He had good reason for hesitation, because he was determined to do something useful—a phrase which constantly recurs in his letters—and not to throw away his life and reputation in vain. He wrote characteristically to Bowring, the secretary of the London Greek Committee, that the Greeks' chief needs were mountain artillery, gunpowder, and medical stores. But the Greeks who called on him at Metaxata set more store by money and his presence with them. Byron was reluctant to commit himself to appearing personally in Greece until the more practical requirements were met. "I really cannot defray the charges of half Greece, and the Frank adventurers besides," he wrote. Nor was he willing to take sides among the Greeks, so they must first settle their own quarrels. He had not yet appreciated how powerful an incentive to unity and to national morale his own presence on Greek soil would be; nor was he conscious how little time he had, often though his mind was preoccupied with early death. He enjoyed discussing religion with the high-minded army doctor, James Kennedy, but this was no substitute for action. A succession of philhellenes tried to stir him from his mood of doubt and self-depreciation.

Apart from Trelawny, there was young Hamilton Brown, whom Byron warmly admired, not least because he was related to Lord Archibald Hamilton. Others who passed through full of enthusiasm, which was to wane sharply in some cases, were James Emerson, Captain Humphreys (on his second tour of service) and Dr. Julius

Millingen. Humphreys became bitter against the Greeks after his second experience of the war, and Millingen actually abandoned them to serve the Turks instead. But at the end of 1823 they were still fired with a spirit of romance, which Byron invariably sought to deflate. To one of the most admirable and disinterested young men who called at Metaxata, George Finlay, later to be renowned as a historian of Greece, he commented with a sardonic insight that Finlay came to share in his old age: "You are young and enthusiastic and therefore sure to be disappointed when you know the Greeks as well as I do." Still, Finlay was determined to be a hero—which indeed he was—and Byron handled him tenderly, being overwhelmed with emotion at his resemblance to the dead Shelley. Finlay moved on early to the mainland in response to Napier's warning that the philhellenes were becoming an embarrassment in Cephallonia. Trelawny also moved on, and so did all the rest. Still Byron stayed.

The most consequential of his callers during his period of delay on the island was Colonel the Hon. Leicester Stanhope, a forty-year-old veteran of the Napoleonic wars. He arrived at Metaxata on his way to Greece, as an emissary of the London Greek Committee, in November 1823. Contemporary criticism, including Byron's own, has labelled Stanhope with unflattering epithets, mainly of a ridiculous character. He was in fact a courageous and enlightened man, though inclined to be despotic and doctrinaire, and not particularly philhellene in sympathy. His dogmas were those of Jeremy Bentham, whom he admired to distraction. Greece to him was simply a virgin ground for trying out the experiments of Benthamism. Few apart from himself knew what this might mean; but the Greeks are a polite race, and they politely agreed with everything he said. Consequently his letters home, which were later collected into a book, give a striking impression of the success of Bentham's doctrines. His object, he declared, was to enable the Greek people to read and contemplate Bentham's works:[1] "Conviction follows". Byron was less easily convinced, and treated him with mockery. Gordon more

[1] Stanhope, *Greece in 1823 and 1824* (London, 1824), p. 90 and *passim.*

charitably wrote that at first the Greeks were mystified,[1] but they were "acute enough speedily to discover the purity of his enthusiasm and to humour his day-dreams".

Benthamite theory required the establishment of utilitarian societies, the improvement of education, the creation of a free press, and above all the adoption of a republican constitution on the model of Switzerland or the U.S.A. Stanhope surprised the Greeks by constantly extolling the merits of the American constitution (in which, of course, he was supported by the American philhellenes) and decrying that of his own country.[2] When Greeks or his fellow-countrymen talked of a kingdom of Greece, he asked them to remember "the corruption and effeminacy, the disorders and convulsions, to which large monarchies are subject, and the stability and grandeur of America". His interest in the Swiss variety of republicanism had naturally led him to visit Switzerland on his way to Greece, and there he called on Count John Capodistrias in Lausanne. Swiss friends convinced him that Capodistrias was not a tool of the Russians, which was gratifying, but Stanhope was somewhat disillusioned by their conversation, which he reported at length.[3] Capodistrias said that:

"... we must not attempt to Anglicanise Greece. I replied that we rather wished to Americanise her. The Count thought our end should be to enlighten Greece, and to act upon utilitarian principles. Yes, said I, Count, but do you think that the *Sainte Alliance* will allow Greece to establish a virtuous republic. His Excellency spoke as well as could be expected; he beat about the bush and then said that it was not in the nature of things that monarchs should encourage republics."

Clearly Capodistrias was not the man for Stanhope's purposes, but they parted with mutual respect.

Stanhope had an unfortunate gift for self-deception. He concluded, quite mistakenly, that all Capodistrias' ideas were "in

[1] Gordon, *History of the Greek Revolution*, vol. II, p. 108.
[2] Stanhope, p. 22; Larrabee, p. 165.
[3] Stanhope, pp. 11–13.

coincidence with our own". It was the same at Berne, where he gave the philhellenic committee a succinct account of the activities of their comrades in Britain, with a strong emphasis on propaganda and public enlightenment.[1] His order of priorities is significant:

"The *Edinburgh* and *Quarterly Reviews* had both ably advocated the cause. The latter had especially recommended the Committee to furnish the Greeks with the means of acquiring knowledge. The Committee had sent out lithographic and other presses to Greece, and hoped soon to hear of their having been instrumental in the diffusion of knowledge. The Committee and the Quakers both contemplated sending out schoolmasters. Two Greek youths were educating by the Foreign School Society, and three schools on the Lancasterian principle were said to have been established in Greece. Mr. Bentham had also directed me to send home two intelligent Greek boys, for the purpose of their being first instructed, and then employed as teachers for the diffusion of useful education. The Committee contemplated sending to Greece many elementary works on education, on the sciences, on agriculture, and on the art of war. Feeling strongly that Greece could not long maintain herself without military discipline, they had been, above all things, anxious to promote that object. They had, for this purpose, sent out to Greece officers of engineers, of artillery, of infantry, and cavalry; also, a most able fire-master, and several mechanics for the manufacture of all the materials of war—cannon, mortars, carriages, arms, Congreve-rockets, Schrapnel-shells, gunpowder, &c."

The Swiss philhellenes were reported to be satisfied, but Byron certainly would not have been, especially as the fire-master (William Parry) and his mechanics proved far from competent, and cavalry officers were almost useless. Byron told Trelawny[2] that what he wanted first was "an engineer and a trumpeter (we have chirurgeons already)".

The comforting belief that "conviction follows" accompanied Stanhope from every encounter. He was delighted with everyone he

[1] Stanhope, p. 8.
[2] Trelawny (ed. Morpurgo), p. 153.

met on his way across Europe. The pleasantest surprise of all came when he arrived in Cephallonia, to find Colonel Napier a "doing man"—his favourite term of approval. So, he thought, was Byron, though not doing much at the moment. Byron did not reciprocate the satisfaction. He wrote to Bowring of Stanhope that "he came up (as they all do who have not been in this country before) with some high-flown notions of the sixth form at Harrow or Eton, but Colonel Napier and I soon set him right". Byron had no interest in his Benthamite enthusiasm; nor did he much care, theoretical republican though he might be, what form of government the Greeks adopted so long as they agreed upon it. Above all, he distrusted Stanhope's plans for setting up a printing-press in Mesolonghi and issuing newspapers and books full of utilitarian doctrines. The "typographical Colonel" was his contemptuous nickname for Stanhope. "It is odd enough," he wrote, "that Stanhope, the soldier, is all for writing down the Turks, whilst I, the writer, am all for fighting them down." The judgement is not unjust. Nor is it to the discredit of either man, for the Greeks needed both their conceptions of freedom. But they needed Byron's first.

All now looked to him for the initiative. His letters show an acute and uncomfortable awareness that he was expected to play a role which he still could not quite comprehend. To be useful was his constant aim: but how? A typical expression of his uncertainty is to be found in a letter to Augusta Leigh[1] in October 1823:

"You ask why I came up amongst the Greeks? It was stated to me that my doing so might tend to their advantage in some measure in their present struggle for independence, both as an individual and as a member for the Committee now in England, How far this may be realised I cannot pretend to anticipate, but I am willing to do what I can."

The same willingness, the same anxiety, the same perplexity, recur again and again in his letters from Cephallonia. Yet still he waited month after month; and still the Greeks and the philhellenes waited upon his decision. Why did he not simply plunge straight into action?

[1] *Letters and Journals*, vol. VI, p. 259.

The reasons are complex, just as his mood was complex in the last year of his life. Some were psychological, and belong rather to his biography than to the story of the philhellenes. They include his sense of weariness, tedium and apathy; his premonitions of an early death; his inability to make the break with Teresa Guiccioli absolutely final, especially with her brother at his side, or to replace her in his wandering affections. Those who remarked how much time he spent debating theology with Dr. James Kennedy, the "Saint", wondered whether the attraction might not lie rather in the charms of his pretty wife; but Kennedy and others who shared their discussions had no doubt of his sincerity. Dr. Kennedy later wrote his *Conversations on Religion with Lord Byron* to clear him of "that obloquy which is attached to his name in the minds of most Christians". His faith in Byron's religious interests was at least supported by the evidence of George Finlay, who was also much in Byron's company in his last months. Though he regarded Kennedy's efforts with amusement, Finlay confirmed that "few people were better acquainted with the Scriptures" than Byron.[1] Such interests as these did not detain him in Cephallonia, but they serve to illuminate his state of mind.

There were other, more practical restraints on his determination. The Greek leaders were still largely an unknown quantity. They could not agree on a national policy or a united command. One of the best of them, Marko Botsaris of Suli, who had been in correspondence with Byron as soon as his arrival in Cephallonia became known, had been killed in action a few days after writing to welcome him. Byron's uncertainty whom to trust led him to make practical enquiries through Hamilton Brown, who left Cephallonia for the Peloponnese in September 1823. He carried Byron's questionnaire, which survives.[2] It is full of sensible enquiries to be put to Kolokotronis and Mavrokordatos' followers: on their numerical strength and rates of pay and the cost of living; on the prisoners they had taken and how they were treated; on their communications

[1] Doris Langley Moore, *The Late Lord Byron* (London, 1961), pp. 338–9, 352.
[2] *Nineteenth Century*, vol. C, p. 408.

with the islands; on the leading personalities and the degree of control they had over their troops. He was also in touch with Hastings at this time, and received from him an embittered report on the Greek leaders, which he endorsed with a reference to Hastings' courage, coolness and enterprise.[1] So he clearly suffered no delusions about the type of Greeks he would have to work with.

He had no better reason to think highly of the support available from London. The loan had not yet arrived, nor did a penny of it come in Byron's lifetime. There was no news yet of the much-vaunted team of explosives experts under William Parry. (As late as the end of January 1824, Byron was still to write:[2] "I presume from the retardment that he is the same Parry who attempted the North Pole and is (it may be supposed) now crossing the South"). It is not surprising that Byron had doubts of the practical judgement of the London Committee. His doubts were justified. Few of them had any idea what was really needed in Greece. Even the notions of the "typographical Colonel" were nearer to reality than those of his colleagues. Their early consignments of stores included, for example, a quantity of Greek Bibles (in a translation which the Greeks denounced as incorrect); a collection of mathematical instruments (on which Byron commented that "none of the Greeks know a problem from a poker"); a bundle of water-colour paintings, and a laboratory. Byron had written a long and practical letter to Bowring as early as May 1823 to tell the London Committee the sort of stores and the type of men that were needed in Greece.[3] But those dogmatic radicals showed little sign of taking his advice. It was small wonder that he hesitated, and dallied in Cephallonia.

While Byron dallied, the newcomers congregated in increasing numbers. Some came to fight, some to execute missions for the London Committee, some out of curiosity. Stanhope reported that there were about twenty British in Mesolonghi early in 1824. Not all their names are known, nor are those of others who were in action

[1] *Nineteenth Century*, vol. C, p. 409.
[2] *Nineteenth Century*, vol. C, p. 407.
[3] *Letters and Journals*, vol. pp. 205–11.

elsewhere. Finlay[1] reports an anonymous ex-midshipman on a Greek ship at Mesolonghi in 1823. A young man from Cambridge, who had enlisted as a Greek soldier, was seen dying in poverty the following year.[2] Among the unexpected tourists in 1823–24 was George Waddington, a Fellow of Trinity College, Cambridge, who wrote in some surprise of the Greeks' suspicious attitude towards him:[3] "That I should be travelling in this country, and at this moment, for mere amusement or curiosity, is, of course, quite incredible." It was indeed; but others were also doing so. Lord Charles Murray, a son of the Duke of Atholl, had no other purpose in mind, though he stayed to join the Greek cause and gave his life for it. Two other English travellers, called Wright and Railton, suffered nothing more severe than capture and robbery by pirates from Ydra. Without doubt there were many other unrecorded visitors to Greece, though Stanhope noted with unreasonable surprise that the former "rage for travelling here" seemed to have diminished.

Apart from the influx of amateur philhellenes, there were also those who might more naturally be described as mercenaries. Not the least mercenary of all was Dr. Julius Millingen, who by all accounts never ceased agitating about his pay, and finally deserted the Greek cause in 1825 for better remuneration from the Egyptian commander, Ibrahim Pasha. But the term more naturally applies to the lower ranks, who were hired by the London Committee for their technical qualifications. Chief among them were the artificers belatedly sent out with William Parry to help him organise a corps of artillery and engineers; together with Hodges, a fire-master, Gill, a fireman, and Fowke, a Clerk of the Works. None of them was inspired by any sentiment of philhellenism, and almost all insisted on being repatriated as soon as they found their lives in danger. But Parry stayed, and earned a certain fame by his devotion to Byron. Almost the only thing about him on which all accounts agree was that he was a heavy drinker. Byron was alone in finding him good

[1] Finlay, *History of Greece*, vol. VI, p. 323.
[2] H. Lytton Bulwer, *An Autumn in Greece* (London. 1826), p. 123.
[3] George Waddington, *A Visit to Greece in 1823 and 1824* (London, 1825), p. 141.

company—"a fine rough subject" he called him—perhaps because he had a talent for mimicry, especially of the Benthamite enthusiasts. His account of *The Last Days of Lord Byron* (1825), though not entirely his own work, was to be a valuable source to later biographers. But his services to the immediate cause were slight.

Such unpromising material and resources in the field justified Byron's long hesitation in Cephallonia. Nevertheless at last, with a certain fatalism, the die was cast. Byron set sail from Cephallonia on 30th December, 1823, and arrived at Mesolonghi, after an adventurous journey (in the course of which he was nearly captured by the Turks and twice escaped shipwreck) on 4th January, 1824. The story of his last three and a half months—all the time that he was allowed to win immortality in Greece, but time enough—has been told so often and in so much detail that no repetition is necessary. The tragedy and disillusion of it are deeply moving; but so are the courage and the glory, which Greeks—the most religious and least blasphemous of peoples—have been disposed to compare to the story of the Resurrection. "I believed myself on a fool's errand from the outset," Byron wrote from Mesolonghi. He described the Greeks as "an intriguing cunning unquiet generation"; and he showed that familiarity with the Scriptures which so impressed Finlay by quoting from St. Paul, in a disparaging sense, the text:[1] "For there is no difference between a Jew and a Greek." But also he wrote: "I must see this Greek business out (or *it me*)."

"Whoever goes into Greece at present should do it as Mrs. Fry went into Newgate—not in the expectation of meeting with any especial indication of existing probity, but in the hope that time and better treatment will reclaim the present burglarious and larcenous tendencies which have followed this General Gaol delivery". Byron wrote thus in his Journal while still in Cephallonia,[2] at the end of September 1823. The passage shows both the accuracy and the humanity of his judgement before setting out on the last stage of his earthly pilgrimage. Unlike so many of his companions, he had no

[1] *Letters and Journals*, vol. VI, p. 271.
[2] *Letters and Journals*, vol. VI, p. 247.

Edward John Trelawny

William Cobbett

David Urquhart

Sir John Bowring

extravagant expectations; but unlike them too, he did not retreat when confronted by the dreadful reality, which he had foreseen and they had not. Nor was it only the Greeks who lived down to his expectations. The foreign philhellenes in Mesolonghi quarrelled with each other; Parry's artificers insisted on being sent home; Stanhope and his fellow-Benthamites upset the Greeks with the provocative contents of their periodicals; Trelawny pursued hare-brained schemes of his own devising, largely animated by jealousy of Byron. Meanwhile Byron himself suffered what was probably an epileptic fit, and sensed his approaching end. To Dr. Kennedy he wrote: "I am not unaware of the precarious state of my health, nor am, nor have ever been deceived on that subject. But it is proper that I should remain in Greece; and it were better to die doing something than nothing."

Stanhope had the same idea, being in his own phrase "a doing man". But one can understand Byron's annoyance with what he was doing. William Parry reports him as saying of Stanhope that:

"he has a plan for organising the military forces, for establishing posts, for regulating the administration of justice, for making Mr. Bentham the apostle of the Greeks, and for whipping little boys in the most approved manner."

Only on the first of these plans could Byron agree with him. Meanwhile he was infuriated to learn that Stanhope had appointed Dr. Meyer—a Swiss republican whom Byron described as a "petty tyrant"—to edit his first newspaper in Mesolonghi, with hideous and predictable conflicts as a result. Stanhope also wrote off to Malta for Bibles in modern Greek, which the good Dr. Kennedy (the Saint, not the Sinner) arranged to forward to Mesolonghi by hand of Parry's artificers. The translation again turned out to be of an unsatisfactory character, which was a further source of trouble. Only with difficulty did Byron frustrate Stanhope's plans for introducing Protestant missionaries as well—a curious ambition for a dedicated Benthamite. But Byron magnanimously undertook to give the Bible Society "as fair play as Mr. Wilberforce himself would". Millingen confirms that he punctiliously did so.[1]

[1] Millingen, p. 19.

To the last Byron clung to his desire to serve, to be useful, and to set an example of leadership and humanity. In a letter written in February 1824 to explain his intention of leading the Greeks against the Turks in person, he gave three reasons why he should go:[1]

"firstly, because they will sooner listen to a foreigner than one of their own people, out of native jealousies: secondly, because the Turks will sooner treat or capitulate (if such occasion should happen) with a Frank than a Greek; and thirdly, because nobody else seems disposed to take the responsibility..."

They were three good reasons, characteristic of his common sense and grasp of realities. Always consistent through pain and disappointment, he continued the quest to be practical, useful and constructive. "I am not come here in search of adventures," he told the romantic Stanhope, "but to assist in the regeneration of a nation." To his banker in Zante he wrote: "I still hope better things, and will stand by the cause so long as my health and circumstances will permit me to be supposed useful." Again he wrote: "I cannot quit Greece while there is a chance of my being of (even supposed) utility"; and again: "I am willing to serve them in any capacity they please, either commanding or commanded–it is much the same to me, as long as I can be of any presumed use to them." In his own phrase, he was "soldier-mad".

A melancholy doubt links all these references to his desire to serve. In every case his usefulness is supposed or presumed–by others. He accepts their belief in him, but cannot translate it into precise terms of action. What was he to do? In what direction was he to exercise the leadership that had been thrust upon him? Much different advice was proffered by those who would have no responsibility for exercising it. All the factions in Greece sought his ear: not only Mavrokordatos, who was with him in Mesolonghi, but Odysseus Androutsos at Athens, Theodore Kolokotronis and Dimitrios Ypsilantis and George Koundouriotis in the Peloponnese. All wanted unity, and each wanted it on his own terms. Some of them had the ear of different philhellenes, who had set out from Mesolonghi

[1] *Letters and Journals*, vol. VI, p. 315.

on journeys of reconnaissance. Stanhope, for instance, had gone to Athens, where he was entranced by the rough brigand, Odysseus. The Benthamite philosophy apparently appealed immediately to Odysseus—"a doing man", as Stanhope at once discovered. Stanhope's letters are comically naïve in praise of Odysseus, who arranged for his benefit a display of democracy in action, promised to allow him to establish printing-presses and a newspaper, and "ordered an ancient temple to be converted into a Museum". The temple, as it happened, was the Parthenon, but this Stanhope did not at first report.[1]

While negotiating with Odysseus over the foundation of a utilitarian society in Athens, and advising the London Committee to send out emigrants to live in Greece (for whose benefit he drew up a draft advertisement on the cost of living), Stanhope also adopted the idea of organising a grand conference of national unity at the small town of Salona (Amphissa), half-way between Athens and Mesolonghi. To this gathering various philhellene emissaries—Finlay, Humphreys, Trelawny—were sent out to convene the rival factions; and Stanhope earnestly begged Byron to bring Mavrokordatos. He himself would bring Odysseus and, of course, a printing-press. He also visited the seat of the provisional government at Nauplia, to persuade the Peloponnesian leaders to take part. He lectured them on Bentham, on the work of the London Committee, and on the advantages of a free press. ("Your works are known and admired here by the few who are educated," he wrote to Bentham).[2] But all was in vain. The Peloponnesians would not come; Mavrokordatos would not come; Stanhope and Trelawny between them could mobilise only a handful of participants at Salona on 21st April, 1824. And already two days earlier, Byron was dead.

The last tragic scene of Byron's life belongs to another story. It is rather the consequences of it that matter to the story of the philhellenes. As the dreadful news spread, at first all was seemliness and

[1] Stanhope, *Greece in 1823 and 1824*, pp. 130, 136.
[2] Stanhope, p. 196.

sorrow. Mavrokordatos decreed three weeks of national mourning. A salute of thirty-seven guns was fired at the funeral, one for each year of his life, and an oration of impressive eloquence was delivered by Trikoupis, a native of Mesolonghi who had lately served as secretary to Lord Guilford in Corfu. Those immediately around Byron were deeply moved by his last agonies, though it must be added that the doctors among them, including young Millingen, contributed a good deal towards aggravating his suffering. Millingen left his own account of the treatment inflicted on Byron.[1] It included bleeding, lunar caustic, purgatives, and a solution of cream of tartar known as "imperial lemonade". Millingen and Byron's Italian doctor then disputed the merits of leeches on the temples, behind the ears and along the jugular vein, as against anti-spasmodic potions of valerian, ether, etc., but both agreed on yet more bleeding. When all was over, Millingen sent in a bill for 200 guineas, on the argument that "Lords do not die every day".

No less repulsive was the conduct of Trelawny, who tried with characteristic disrespect for the dead to obtain a private view of the corpse in order to satisfy his curiosity about Byron's crippled leg. He claimed to have succeeded, but this was probably a lie. Like Stanhope he found appropriate words of lamentation, but both were really jealous of the dead hero, as their later comments too clearly showed. More attractive and sincere were the words of the Earl of Guilford in a letter to Earl Bathurst from Corfu:[2]

"You have no idea of the grief which Lord Byron's death has occasioned here. His conduct in Greece had been admirable, and his loss is irreparable, as he was the most strenuous supporter of moderate and rational principles. Had he lived longer, all his eccentricities would have been entirely forgotten . . ."

Further afield from Mesolonghi, the news was received with emotions which might have surprised Byron in his lifetime. He could have counted on being mourned by his literary friends, like Scott and Moore. But he could have known nothing of the young

[1] Millingen, p. 128.

[2] *Nineteenth Century*, vol. C, p. 400.

Benjamin Disraeli, who copied his style of dress, took on his Venetian gondolier, and consciously modelled himself on Byronism; nor of the still younger Alfred Tennyson, who was so stunned by the news that he went about all day crying: "Byron is dead! Byron is dead!"

Byron would have been even more surprised by some of his obituary notices. *The Times* wrote:

"That noblest of enterprises, the deliverance of Greece, employed the whole of Lord Byron's latter days – of his pecuniary resources, and of his masculine spirit. It was a cause worthy of a poet and a hero ..."

Such reactions to the drama of Mesolonghi were important, because they were to be reflected in a growing sense of public indignation at the British government's apparent indifference to the fate of the Greeks. Within three and a half years, the outcome was to be settled in the bay of Navarino, on 20th October, 1827. But the long lapse of time shows that the sense of indignation was slow to accumulate political force. In the meantime the reaction of the Establishment to the death of Byron was perhaps more accurately expressed in another obituary notice, published in *John Bull*:

"He has ... quitted the world at the most unfortunate period of his career, and in the most unsatisfactory manner – in voluntary exile, when his mind, debased by evil associations, and the malignant brooding over imaginary ills, has been devoted to the construction of elaborate lampoons."

The British public was in fact going through what Macaulay was to call a few years later "one of its periodical fits of morality". However shocked it might be by the thought of a peer of the realm dying in a Turkish fishing village in the most disreputable company, it soon returned to its true form. So, unfortunately, did those round Byron, both philhellenes and Greeks. They bickered over his reputation, his policies, his literary remains, his money, and even his corpse. The Greeks reverted to civil war, which lasted more than a year, off and on, until the pressure of their enemies drove them together again at the eleventh hour. The philhellenes were demoralised by

Byron's death. Such unity of purpose as there had ever been among them vanished overnight. When Mesolonghi fell to the Turks two years after Byron's death, it seemed only the final blow in a cause that was already lost. For the intervening disasters Byron can bear no blame, though some of his companions were not above trying to blame him.

Stanhope and Trelawny became the ringleaders in belittling Byron's services in order to enhance their own. Many of the philhellenes departed for home, and others who were on their way turned back. Almost all those who had known Byron competed with each other in producing mendacious and egocentric memoirs of him. But less sophisticated souls displayed more sincere and admirable feeling. Byron's valet, William Fletcher, once a Nottinghamshire farm-hand, who had reluctantly accompanied him twice to these out-landish parts, wrote of his master to his publisher, John Murray: "... I Scearsely Now what I either Say or Do for after 20 Years Service To My Lord he was More to me than a father and I am too much Distressed to now Give a Correct accompt Of every Per-tickeler which I hope to Do at my arrival in England ..." The same feelings were expressed by an old Rumeliot whom James Emerson met[1] in 1825: "he came and he gave his counsels, and his fortune, and his life; and when he died, we felt like men suddenly struck with blindness, when the only thing that could equal our sorrow for his loss, was our perplexity for the future."

Scores of such stories could be cited to show that it has been the same from that day to this. Two will suffice. A year or two after Byron's death, a young American surgeon, lately graduated from Harvard, was crossing the Gulf of Salamis in a boat with a rough mountain captain and his men:[2]

"... I pulled out a volume of Byron's works, and was reading. The wind blowing open the leaves, the captain caught a glimpse of the portrait and recognised it. He begged to take the book, and

[1] Emerson and others, *A Picture of Greece in 1825*, vol. I, p. 109.

[2] Samuel G. Howe, *An Historical Sketch of the Greek Revolution* (ed. G. G. Arnakis: Austin Texas, 1966), part I, p. 203, footnote.

looking for a moment with melancholy at the face of the noble lord, he kissed it and passed it to his men who did the same, saying: 'He was great and good'."

That is not the end of the story. More than a century later, in the days when Greeks adopted mythological and historical names to hide their identity during the resistance to Nazi occupation, a young Englishman was escorted about the streets of Athens under guard by a young Greek calling himself "Vyronas". When asked why he chose that name, he replied in the same words. It has always seemed strange to the Greeks, as it has to Italians, Frenchmen, Germans and other Europeans, that the English have mostly failed to recognise in Byron their greatest countryman of the 19th century.

CHAPTER V

The Achievement of Independence

WITH THE DEATH of Byron, the glory was departed, and so were the faint-hearted philhellenes. The Greeks then learned who were their true friends. Only a handful stayed throughout the war of independence from beginning to end. Outstanding among them were Frank Abney Hastings, Captain Hane, and George Finlay, who left their posts in the front line only for a time in 1825–26 in quest of new recruits or equipment in western Europe. Next to them in a place of honour stands Captain Hamilton of the *Cambrian*: he was kept in Greek waters by his duty as a naval officer, but he frequently went beyond the call of duty in his humanitarian services to the Greeks. Trelawny also had no intention of deserting the Greeks until compelled to do so, though his conduct was often erratic and of doubtful value to the Greeks. He attached himself to Odysseus, who periodically retired from the fighting and made an "accommodation" (known to the Greeks as a *kapáki*) with the Turks. The two ambiguous heroes spent much of their time in a cave high up on Mount Parnassus, which Odysseus had fortified as a precaution against his enemies; and there Trelawny lived intermittently with the brigand chieftain's half-sister, a child of thirteen, as his wife. Of the rest, little can be said to their credit.

The year 1824 was an unhappy one for all concerned in the war. Many had gone: Parry and his artisans, as well as Stanhope and Emerson. At least two – Blackett and Winter – committed suicide in the latter part of the year. It is not known why, but medical research a century later has established that the area immediately north of the Gulf of Corinth is afflicted with a peculiarly virulent type of malaria which produces acute depression in its victims.[1] Dr. Millingen himself was seriously ill in 1824, and barely survived. He was nursed back to health by a young newcomer, Lord Charles Murray, a son of the Duke of Atholl, who had come to Greece on the Grand Tour and stayed to join the philhellenes. "To my astonishment," he declared, "I find myself at once called to take part in what is passing around me." But it was not for long: a few weeks later he in turn fell sick, and died, in August 1824, universally lamented for his generosity and disinterestedness.[2] Other new arrivals in the same year were to leave a less savoury reputation behind them: notably a genteel, romantic and perhaps soft-headed English officer, Captain H. G. Whitcombe, and a young Scot, Captain William Fenton, who both fell into the network of Greek intrigues.

These newcomers had to be maintained, if not paid; and still not a penny of the London loan had been received. The London Committee had to act fast if the cause was not to collapse altogether. Blaquière arrived in April 1824, a few days after Byron's death, with the first instalment of the loan, and stayed in Greece till May 1827. But the bankers in Zante with whom the money was deposited decided that the death of Byron had invalidated the commission to dispense the money, so Blaquière was unable to make any payments till new commissioners arrived. At the same time Stanhope, one of the original commissioners, was recalled to England by the War Office. He left in June 1824, mystifying the Greeks to the last with his parting words. This life-long republican assured them that he had no alternative:

"The king, my sovereign, has commanded me immediately to return to England. I obey the royal mandate."

He departed happy in the conviction that he had left behind him a permanent memorial in the postal services, newspapers and utilitarian societies which he had founded. "By my warm attachment to the Greek cause, my resolution in avoiding all factions, and my open

[1] British officers serving in the same area in 1942–4 suffered particularly from this sickness; and at least one committed suicide while convalescent.

[2] Millingen, pp. 156, 182–3.

conduct, I have gained friends on all sides," he wrote.[1] Others took a less optimistic view.

Meanwhile new commissioners were on their way to Greece to administer the loan. Gordon and Hobhouse had both refused to serve. Of the two who replaced them, one already knew the Greeks well: this was J. Hamilton Brown, whom Maitland had removed from the Ionian Islands for his philhellene sympathies. He had accompanied Byron to Cephallonia and preceded him to Greece; then returned to England with the Greek deputies to help them secure the loan. His companion on his second visit to Greece in August 1824 was a newcomer: Henry Lytton Bulwer, the elder brother of the celebrated novelist, later a diplomatist in Washington and Constantinople. At this stage of his remarkable and often eccentric career, he was a classic type of the young romantic philhellene, whom Byron had ridiculed but also passionately inspired. The book which he wrote about his experiences, *An Autumn in Greece*, is full of the language of Byron: his Albanians, of course, are complete "with their snowy camiss and their shaggy capote"; and he could recognise, like Byron, in the modern Greek "that image of Liberty which . . . was cherished in his heart". But his enthusiasm was still that of the sixth-form schoolboy which so irritated Byron.[2]

Inevitably Greece reminded him of his old school:[3]

"There is that in this country, which amply repays one the trouble, if I do not say danger, of visiting it: – all we meet is fresh, and unlike what we ever saw before. The dress, the manners, the very ignorance of the people has something in it wild and original. We are brought back to our boyhood by the very name of Greece; and every spot in this beautiful land reminds us of the days devoted to its classic fables, and the scenes where we were taught them. Methinks I see old Harrow Churchyard, and its venerable yews, under whose shadows I have lain many a summer evening."

[1] Stanhope, *Greece in 1823 and 1824*, p. 159.
[2] Bulwer, *An Autumn in Greece*, pp. 4, 45.
[3] Bulwer, pp. 62, 89, 92.

But still the Greeks seemed to him unworthy of their heritage. "These people have no grand views, no conception of a straightforward, honest and consistent conduct; all is to be done by trick and artifice; they are the very reverse of the old Romans . . ." (Had he noticed that they actually called themselves Romans?) His judgement vacillated, however. There were times when "the great mass of Greek population appeared to me far better than I had expected to find it, or than it is generally considered". He found "brave sailors, enterprising merchants, and a hardy peasantry". The deterioration of the Greeks was exaggerated; yet "those who look back to the classic days of Greece, would be greatly disappointed at its present state".

The ambivalence of Bulwer's judgements shows that Byron's work for the cause of truth had been half undone, but only half. The newcomers had not reverted to the complacent contempt of Gell or Dodwell, but they had still not learned to accept the Greeks as an independent people either. The old epithets regularly recur. The Greeks were still semi-barbarous, self-opinionated, vain, greedy, suspicious, dishonest: all these terms are to be found in the writings of the middle 1820s as well as twenty years before. But the situation was now very different. Bulwer asserted categorically that there was no possibility of the Greeks reverting to subjection under the Turks. He speculated confidently on their future system of government as an independent power, and adjudged Leopold of Saxe-Coburg an acceptable sovereign.[1] (The speculation is interesting, when it is recalled that nearly forty years later he angled for the throne of Greece himself, when it fell vacant in 1862). But his hopes of contributing actively to the cause himself were cut short when he was taken ill, as also was his companion, Hamilton Brown; and both returned to England a year after their arrival.

Many others came and went during the bleak year, 1824, but almost all were filled with doubts about the prospects of the Greeks and few of them contributed much to the cause. Humphreys returned in January 1824 and stayed for more than a year this time,

[1] Bulwer, pp. 260, 346.

becoming more and more disillusioned.[1] "The Greeks are in a state of the lowest moral degradation," he wrote, though the nature of his criticisms was somewhat inconsequent and even inconsistent. "The generality of the lower orders are excessively ugly," he found. The islanders were the best of them all, the Moreots or people of the Peloponnese were the worst:

"inhospitable, intractable, stubborn and cowardly . . . insensible to kindness . . . penurious and dirty . . . dishonest in their dealings, their natural acuteness and intelligence of disposition are exercised only to deceive."

Humphreys' catalogue of woes reached its climax when he witnessed the fate of two captured Turks, who were "staked and burnt alive"; followed on the very next page by the loss of his Newfoundland dog to an accidental bullet. "It was a disgusting service," he concluded, "and I determined to leave it as soon as the campaign should be over." When he left the country late in 1825, he doubted if the Greeks could survive; but nevertheless he was back again a year later, and died on Greek soil in 1826.

James Emerson (later Sir James Emerson Tennent) had been disillusioned by the Greeks even earlier than Humphreys, and left Greece soon after Byron's death. But he too returned in 1825, this time as a war correspondent for *The Times*; and he asserted against all the evidence that "of the ultimate success of the Greek Revolution, be it soon or late, I see no reason to doubt." Though he was disgusted like Humphreys at the sight of a massacre of Turkish prisoners on the island of Ydra,[2] he also took part in more honourable actions under Admiral Miaoulis at sea and under Makriyannis on land. In the celebrated battle at the Mills of Lerna on 25th June, 1825, in which Makriyannis inflicted a first defeat on the Sultan's Egyptian troops, Emerson fought alongside his future brother-in-law, Robert James Tennent, who was also a war correspondent for the *Globe and Traveller*. He was lucky in the company in which he

[1] Humphreys, *Journal of a Visit to Greece*, (vol. II of *A Picture of Greece in 1825*) pp. 239–40, 310–11, 337.
[2] Finlay, vol. VI, p. 354.

fought, for Makriyannis was the most selfless of the *kapetánioi* on land; and at sea Miaoulis was his equal in sterling patriotism, as Emerson warmly recognised.[1]

Idealism and heroism were not dead among the philhellenes, even though Dr. Millingen deserted them for the Turkish service at about the same time. Caught among the garrison at Navarino when the Egyptians besieged it, he arranged a private surrender for himself, his servant and his baggage, which he "justified by the natural law of self-preservation". Another consideration was that he found the Egyptian commander, Ibrahim Pasha, a more reliable paymaster than the Greeks.[2] At least he did not allow himself to become bitter against the Greeks, whom he warmly praised in his *Memoirs* as intelligent, industrious, hardy and indefatigable, and also as graceful, fluent and friendly.[3] From a notorious Turcophil, such as he became, this is high praise. He was fortunately the only renegade during the war, though there were plenty of less worthy characters attracted to Greece by Byron's fame: "a host of travellers, speculators, men of all fortunes and descriptions", according to Bulwer.[4] Little is known of them: in most cases, not even their names; nor is it any loss.

If possible, the year 1825 was even more depressing than 1824. Demoralisation among the philhellenes showed itself in personal quarrels, intrigues, suicides, even some outbreaks of sheer lunacy. The strangest episode, in which all the symptoms of derangement and black comedy found their meeting-point, was the attempt to murder Trelawny in June 1825. Although the motives of the plot are lost in obscurity, they were almost certainly political as well as personal. Trelawny was living in Odysseus' cave high up in Mount Parnassus, accompanied by his girl-wife, a Hungarian servant, the young Scottish Captain William Fenton, and a miscellaneous bodyguard of Greek *pallikária* (heroes or thugs, according to taste), such as accompanied every self-respecting *kapetánios*. Odysseus was not with him: indeed, Odysseus was engaged in one of his periodical

[1] Emerson, vol. I, pp. 173–5, pp. 351 seq.

[2] Millingen, pp. 323–31.

[3] Millingen, p. 158 seq.

[4] *An Autumn in Greece*, p. 306.

intrigues with the Turks, from which Trelawny hoped to rescue him. But Odysseus' political rivals, particularly Mavrokordatos, considered Trelawny's friendship with him dangerous. They plotted to murder Trelawny, with the connivance of the American soldier of fortune, George Jarvis, and Captain Fenton. The weak-minded young Englishman, Captain Whitcombe, was also involved in the plot. The story of it is known in some detail, partly from Trelawny's own reminiscences and also from those of Humphreys, who had it from Trelawny a few weeks after the event.[1]

The attempt was made early in June, when first Fenton (whom Emerson described as "totally divested of every principle or feeling of a gentleman", and Gordon as "a determined villain")[2] and then Whitcombe had joined Trelawny at Odysseus' cave. One afternoon Fenton suggested a shooting match. While Trelawny was taking aim two shots hit him in the back. The first was certainly fired by Whitcombe, the second probably by Fenton. Both men tried at once to run away, but Fenton was killed by Trelawny's Hungarian servant and Whitcombe was caught by his bodyguard. He protested his innocence, and Trelawny, who was badly wounded but not unconscious, prevented his men from an immediate execution. The story he extracted from Whitcombe was that Fenton had persuaded him, under the influence of drink, that the salvation of Greece required Trelawny's death. Independent witnesses of undoubted integrity, such as Dr. Howe, Gordon and Finlay, later had documentary evidence (which has not survived) that Jarvis, Fenton and Mavrokordatos were all parties to the conspiracy. Jarvis, who had once called Fenton his only friend in Greece, later regretted "having had the least acquaintance" with him;[3] but never satisfactorily explained his own role in the attempted murder. Trelawny survived the attempt on his life partly because of his own natural strength and partly through the devotion of his friends. Humphreys hurried to his assistance; so did Captain Hamilton of the *Cambrian*, who sent him a

[1] Trelawny, pp. 189–95; Humphreys, pp. 280–1.
[2] Emerson, vol. I, p. 275; Gordon, vol. II, p. 187.
[3] Larrabee, *Hellas Observed*, p. 101.

medical officer and embarked him on a sloop, to take him to the Ionian Islands.

This tragic and scandalous episode showed how deeply some of the philhellenes had become involved in Greek intrigues. Nor was the unsavoury story finished. Though Trelawny survived, his friend Odysseus perished—almost certainly murdered in captivity on the Acropolis at Athens, whether or not on Mavrokordatos' orders. Humphreys, while trying to organise the rescue of Trelawny, was also taken prisoner by Greek soldiers, for which he bitterly blamed Mavrokordatos. He was held only for a short time, and when released he too returned to England. He wrote himself[1] that "there is not a mountain village in all Greece where the name of an Englishman does not command peculiar deference and attention"; but the same respect was not held by the Greeks' political leaders. Such things would never have happened in Byron's lifetime: the spell of his name was too powerful; and neither the philhellenes nor the Greeks would then have descended to such utterly degraded conduct. There is something ominous about the insane actions of Fenton and Whitcombe the intrigues and feuds of Trelawny, the cowardice of Millingen, the breakdown and suicide of several others, all of which suggest a collapse of the moral basis of philhellenism in the field in 1825.

The year leaves a depressingly blank page in the story of the philhellenes. The deaths, the quarrels, the defections, the departures were compensated by few new arrivals, and scarcely any of those few were sent by the London Greek Committee. Young Dr. Howe[2] arrived fresh from Harvard at the beginning of the year; and Edward Masson, a Scottish schoolmaster, came to set up a model school for the little Greeks on Ydra. Both became highly respected and beloved; but the London Greek Committee could claim no credit for either. It was characteristic of the changing situation that the new men of 1825, few as they were, belonged to a new type, no longer

[1] Humphreys, p. 293.
[2] Howe's services to Greece in war and peace entitle him to honour in his own right,and not merely as the husband of Julia Ward Howe, who wrote the "Battle Hymn of the Republic".

seeking merely warlike adventures. The surgeon, the school-master, the newspaper correspondent, had not come deliberately to involve themselves in bloodshed and violence—though all of them inevitably saw action as well—but to witness and perhaps to help in the creation of a new society. In a sense their interest was premature, and many of their hopes were to be disappointed. The absence of any corresponding activity by the London Greek Committee during 1825 was not due to apathy or defeatism, but to a more realistic assessment of the immediate prospect.

Advice from the field had convinced the Committee that the Greeks could not win merely by guerrilla warfare on land and piracy at sea. Victory would only come when they had regular, disciplined forces. Their first-hand advisers were divided on the priorities: should efforts be concentrated first on the army or the navy? The professional soldiers among them, such as Gordon, Napier, and Church, naturally urged the priority of the army: only Stanhope, who hardly counted, took the eccentric view that guerrilla warfare was enough provided it were supported by printing-presses and utilitarian societies. Napier, who had arrived in England early in 1824 with a letter of recommendation from Byron, was particularly enthusiastic for a regular army. He claimed that with a sum of £40,000 he could raise a Greek force armed with English rifles, which would take Salonica in a month and Constantinople within two. Although he elaborated these ideas in a pamphlet, "Greece in 1824", and wrote another memorandum two years later outlining the tactics to be employed against Ibrahim Pasha,[1] he did not carry conviction, nor could he persuade the War Office to release him to undertake the command. He returned to Cephallonia in 1825, to resume his long-drawn-out feud with the High Commissioner, Sir Frederick Adam.

This was not quite the end of Napier's active interest in Greece. He was approached again in the summer of 1825 by Mavrokordatos, who sent the young Spyridon Trikoupis—the former secretary of Lord Guilford and panegyrist of Byron—to see him in Cephallonia.

[1] Text in Finlay, *History of Greece*, vol. VII, 340–2.

James Emerson Tennent

Joseph Hume

Sir Edward Codrington

Charles James Napier

But although the Greeks accepted his onerous terms in principle, nothing came of the negotiations. Some of his comments at this time suggest that it may have been just as well. He told Trelawny that he would not go to Greece "without two European regiments, money in hand to pay them, and a portable gallows". Later he wrote that he could never have accepted a command (as did Church) in which he would have been "obliged to beg of his soldiers to do their duty as a personal favour". Although the negotiations with him continued in a desultory way throughout 1826, and his appointment in the Ionian Islands continued until 1830, his destiny—an abstraction in which he passionately believed—was to deny him the glory of liberating Greece, and to lead him to fame elsewhere. "*Peccavi*", he is said to have telegraphed to London when he captured Sind; and perhaps the admission ("I have sinned"), though not the pun, could have been applied to the opportunity he missed in Greece.

Other British advocates of a regular army were also disappointed. Church and Gordon were both approached by the Greek deputies in London, but to no avail; so were Count Nugent and Sir Robert Wilson, two able officers of the Napoleonic wars. Rival pressures and divisions among the British philhellenes conspired to frustrate these tentative negotiations. The French were already active in the same field, and forestalled the London Committee by securing the appointment of the Buonapartist Colonel Fabvier as commander of the Greek regular troops on land. Though a skilled and dedicated officer, his efforts to organise a disciplined force were frustrated by the hostility of the guerrilla chieftains; but for the time being there was no point in trying to appoint a rival British commander-in-chief. The London Greek Committee therefore turned its attention to the naval arm, in favour of which there was an even more powerful lobby among the philhellenes. The enthusiasm of Captain Frank Hastings was supported, though more cautiously, by Captain Hamilton of the *Cambrian*, in command of the squadron in the Aegean. Blaquière, with the somewhat doubtful credit of a merchant sea-captain, urged the same view. It was natural in any case for the British supporters of the Greek cause to assert a national primacy at sea, especially when the French had already established their primacy on land.

As early as 1824, the naval lobby among the pro-English faction of the Greeks and their British supporters had been pressing for the appointment of Lord Cochrane to the command at sea. Cochrane, who was commanding the Brazilian navy at the time, was a brilliant seaman whose eccentricities had already made him a legend. As a junior officer in the Royal Navy, he had persistently quarrelled with his superiors and deliberately infuriated them by drawing attention to his own superior talents. He had won sensational successes in small-scale actions against the French and Spanish fleets in the Napoleonic Wars, taking more in prize-money than any officer in the history of the Royal Navy – £75,000 in the year 1805 alone. His tactical and technical innovations in naval warfare were of a kind peculiarly suited to the sort of operations to which most of his career was devoted, rather than to major fleet actions. Naval mines or torpedoes, fireships, devices for launching propaganda leaflets, kites to accelerate sailing speed, and even poison gas, were among his innovations in the art of war. His genius was equally fertile in civil inventions: among them, oil-lamps for street-lighting, the use of air pressure in tunnelling, and the introduction of bitumen from Trinidad to pave the streets with asphalt. As a radical M.P. he was equally ingenious and impatient of obstruction.

To his naval superiors he was inevitably obnoxious, and this proved his downfall. His first court-martial for indiscipline came in 1798, when he was only twenty-three. Lord St. Vincent described him at this time as "mad, romantic, money-getting and not truth-telling" – four epithets which were often to be repeated. In 1808, after being briefly appointed to a command based on Corfu, he was recalled by Lord Collingwood for "want of discretion". A year later he provoked a court-martial of his commander-in-chief, Lord Gambier, by opposing a vote of thanks to him in the House of Commons; but Gambier was acquitted, and Cochrane was put on half-pay. While out of employment, he pursued all sorts of radical causes with reckless enthusiasm. When Sir Francis Burdett was committed to the Tower of London in 1810 for contempt of the House of Commons, Cochrane—his colleague as M.P. for Westminster—helped him to barricade his house and defend it for two days against a military force. His investigations into the scandals of naval administration led to his arrest in Malta on a ridiculous charge of stealing an official paper, but the authorities connived at his escape. He espoused all the progressive causes of his day (though doubtful about Catholic emancipation), and probably the extravagant vehemence of his support did something to delay them. After a runaway marriage at Gretna Green and other characteristic adventures, his spectacular career came at last to what seemed a final catastrophe when he was involved—foolishly but almost certainly by accident—in a swindle on the Stock Exchange based on a fabricated report of Napoleon's death in 1814. Almost no indignity was spared him: heavily fined, imprisoned, sentenced to the stocks (but reprieved at least from this humiliation), expelled from the House of Commons, deprived of the K.C.B., cashiered from the Royal Navy—it is not surprising that he shook the dust of England off his feet.

The new career which led eventually to his appointment in Greece began in 1818, when he was invited to Chile to command the rebel fleet in the War of Independence against Spain. His brilliant successes in the Chilean service led to similar appointments in Peru and Brazil. For five years he displayed a genius for privateering unexampled since the days of Francis Drake. As usual, however, he provoked violent antagonisms. The British government predictably pursued its vendetta against him by passing the Foreign Enlistment Act of 1819, which was to prove a thorn in the flesh of many British adventurers (including Cecil Rhodes at the time of the Jameson Raid). He quarrelled also with those he was helping to liberate, including San Martin in Peru and the Emperor of Brazil. With all of them he drove a hard bargain over the financial terms on which he was prepared to sell his services. Finally, in 1824, he resigned his command in Brazil, but only when he was sure that he could get the Greek command on satisfactory terms instead.

He returned to England in June 1825 with a legendary reputation which had already dazzled the Greeks. Immediately upon his arrival, he was approached by Hastings, who was in England trying to negotiate the purchase of one or more steamships for use in Greek waters. The idea could be expected to appeal to Cochrane's taste for innovation, for no steamship had yet been put into service by any navy in the world. The pressure was increased a few weeks later with the arrival in London of Dimitrios Miaoulis, brother of the Greek Admiral, who brought a document called the Act of Submission to England, signed by many of the leading Greeks, and accompanied by Captain Humphreys as his interpreter. Canning, who was now Foreign Secretary, adopted the correct attitude of refusing to receive Miaoulis or his petition; but he resisted pressure within the cabinet to prevent Cochrane from going to Greece if he wished. It was Cochrane himself who delayed matters by his determination, as always, to sell his services dearly.

The Greek deputies had arrived in London in August 1824, with orders to purchase eight frigates. They ordered two in America through the New York Greek Committee, and authorised Messrs. Ricardo as their agents to purchase and equip a steamship in London. They had authority to order two such vessels, but claimed that their funds would run to one only. It was to be a corvette of 400 tons named the *Perseverance* (in Greek, *Kartería*), costing £10,000. The engines were to be provided by a Scottish engineer, Alexander Galloway, whose son was unfortunately under contract at the same time to the Viceroy of Egypt, while Hastings undertook to provide the armament at his own expense. As soon as it became known that Cochrane might be available, more ambitious plans were laid. The London Greek Committee was induced by Ellice, Burdett and Hobhouse to put virtually all its funds—some £150,000—at their disposal to hire Cochrane's services and equip a fleet of five more steamships for his use. More than one third of the total sum, amounting to £57,000, was to go into Cochrane's own pocket. As his biographer remarked,[1] "Cochrane's altruism towards Greece rested on a firm financial footing."

[1] Warren Tute, *Cochrane–A Life of Admiral the Earl of Dundonald* (London, 1965), pp. 238–9.

Cochrane's mercenary spirit was not subjected to any effective check by the London Greek Committee, who had come to look upon his services as indispensable. Most of the eighty-odd members of the Committee were content to leave the management of their affairs in the hands of an active minority. The minority included Hobhouse, Ellice, Hume, Burdett, Bowring, Blaquière and Messrs. Ricardo (though David Ricardo, the economist, had died in 1823). Some of them made a handsome profit for themselves out of the Greek loans; none of them, businessmen though they might be, attempted to impose any financial discipline on the transactions entered upon to meet Cochrane's requirements. He ordered what he wanted with no regard to the difficulties of technical innovation and delivery-dates. When things went wrong, he blamed whoever was nearest to hand, usually Hobhouse, Burdett or Ellice. There is no doubt that they were much to blame for inefficiency and carelessness, but so was Cochrane for the casual arrogance with which he expected impossible requirements to be met without adequate supervision.

By 1826 philhellenism was at a low ebb in England, as was noted by the Swiss banker, J. G. Eynard, on a visit to London. It was due at least in part to the disrepute into which the London Greek Committee had fallen, not undeservedly. At a public meeting of the bondholders in September 1826, under the chairmanship of Leicester Stanhope, strong criticisms were expressed. *The Times* described the report presented to the meeting as "a timid compromise between peculation, indolence and incapacity"; and these expressions were not too strong for the facts. Meetings of the Committee itself were now sparsely attended, and soon they ceased to take place altogether. It is hardly surprising that the story of the ships ordered for Greece makes sorry reading, which can be briefly summarised.[1]

Of the two sailing ships ordered in America, one had to be sold before completion in order to pay for the other, which was launched as the *Hope* and renamed the *Hellas*. She became the flagship of the Greek fleet, and ended her career tragically in the harbour of Poros, when Admiral Miaoulis himself blew her up in August 1831 rather

[1] Dakin, pp. 113–127; Virginia Penn in *The Slavonic Review*, vol. XIV (1935–6), pp. 653–6.

than surrender to a Russian Admiral acting on behalf of the Greek government. Of the steamships ordered in England, the *Perseverance* (*Kartería*) was the first in action in Greek waters, where she achieved devastating successes under Hastings' command. The others were so much delayed – in some cases deliberately, by Galloway's dilatory methods – that even those which eventually reached Greece contributed little to the decisive fighting. Cochrane himself could not wait for a British-built ship to command if he was to make an appearance in the Mediterranean at all. A French brig, the *Sauveur*, had to be bought for his personal use at Marseille. He appointed as its captain George Thomas, an Irishman in the Royal Navy, and sailed to Greece accompanied by two smaller ships and a considerable contingent of young adventurers, in February 1827. Meanwhile the terms of his appointment were still under negotiation, and it was not until April that the Greek National Assembly appointed him commander-in-chief of its small and scattered naval forces, among which Hastings' *Kartería* was already the most significant.

It was a historic moment of revival in Greece's fortunes, which had been continuously in decline since Mesolonghi fell to the Turkish and Egyptian forces in April 1826. The revival was marked by a series of seemingly unrelated events. First, the great powers had begun to renew negotiations with a view to ending the ghastly hostilities. Meanwhile the pro-English party had gained ground in Greece, with the result that the same meeting of the National Assembly which appointed Cochrane also invited Church to become commander-in-chief of the land forces. At the same time, as compensation to the pro-Russian faction, Capodistrias was elected provisional President (*Kyvernítis*) of the Greek republic. The Tsar of Russia was already preparing a more active intervention, though no longer under the influence of Capodistrias, and a Russian fleet was to appear in the Mediterranean a few months later. French and British fleets were already there, both commanded by reluctant and critical philhellenes who denied being anything of the kind. A more important arrival, as it turned out, than either Cochrane or Church, was that of the new commander-in-chief of the Mediterranean Fleet,

Vice-Admiral Sir Edward Codrington, who took up his post in February 1827. His eighteen months' tenure of the post was to revolutionise the history of the eastern Mediterranean. In comparison with his unwitting contribution to Greek independence, that of all the rest of the philhellenes put together was negligible; though it may be said with confidence that without Byron at Mesolonghi there could have been no Codrington at Navarino.

The revival of Greece's prospects stimulated a fresh wave of combatant philhellenes. When Hastings brought the *Kartería* to Greece towards the end of 1826, he had with him the faithful Captain Hane in charge of the armaments and at least four British officers new to the struggle (one of them, Lieutenant William Scanlan, an Irishman); and he was joined by the Scottish George Finlay and the American Dr. Howe as ship's surgeon. Humphreys and Gordon had also returned earlier in the same year (Humphreys to die soon afterwards in Aegina). In the following year a new influx accompanied Church and Cochrane, in which the predominance of Irish and Scots was again marked. Church, who was born in Ireland, had with him an Irish A.D.C., Captain Charles O'Fallon, and an Irish sea-captain, Francis Castle, as well as other officers whose names (Francis Kirkpatrick and Gibbon Fitz-Gibbon) suggest an Irish origin. Cochrane also was supported by his fellow-countrymen, including his nephew George Cochrane, and the Urquhart brothers, David and Charles Gordon. To the list of Scots philhellenes active at this time must also be added George Finlay's brother Kirkman, and Edward Masson, the young schoolmaster whom Cochrane persuaded to become his interpreter and Secretary to the Greek Navy. To the Irish must be added Cochrane's captain, George Thomas, and the indefatigably helpful Captain Hamilton, whose unofficial diplomacy was at least partly responsible for the Act of Submission which Miaoulis and Humphreys had carried to London in 1825. At one time it seemed possible that an even larger number of Irishmen might have flooded into Greece, for an American adventurer called William T. Washington (distantly related to his great namesake, and therefore hugely welcome to the Greeks) arrived on Ydra in 1825 with a scheme for recruiting three to four thousand men in Ireland. But his wild notions, which included denunciation of his U.S. citizenship and passionate adherence to the French Royalists, ended predictably in no effect.

Of them all, the one on whom the highest hopes were fastened was Cochrane; but he was also the one who cared least about the Greeks. He felt only a diffused and generalised interest in the independence of oppressed nations anywhere in the world, coupled with a much stronger and more particularised interest in his own pocket. His eccentricities, his arrogant and quarrelsome character, have already been described, and were to be in evidence again in Greece. Even his enthusiasm for liberal causes was tinged with contempt as well as mercenary greed. While in Chile he had delivered himself of a characteristic justification in correspondence with the Spanish Viceroy, to whom he wrote that "a British nobleman had a right to assist any country which was endeavouring to re-establish the rights of aggrieved humanity". As with Byron, no one was allowed to forget his own nobility or the condescension with which he put it at the disposal of lesser breeds. Towards the Greeks he was even more scornful than towards the Latin Americans. For the North Americans, on the other hand, he had a high regard: three of them, including a negro, were in his crew in Greek waters.

Although he set out for Greece with considerable hesitation, he boasted extravagantly of what he intended to do. "The task that now remains is easy," he assured the Greeks in his first address to them: "The fate of the Acropolis is no longer doubtful." (As a matter of fact, the Acropolis was captured by the Turks a few weeks after Cochrane set foot on the soil of Attica, and a large measure of the blame, by common consent, was his.) He repeatedly expressed his impatience to dine on the Acropolis; he promised even to hoist the Greek flag on the Church of Sancta Sophia in Constantinople and to restore the Byzantine Empire. To the Viceroy of Egypt he wrote a threatening letter advising him to divert his energies to cutting a canal through the isthmus of Suez. His letters and speeches were full of literary allusions: Mehmet Ali was advised to study the thirty-first chapter of Isaiah, and the Greeks to read Demosthenes' First Philippic. All this fanfaronade led to very little action on Cochrane's part, except for the bravado of leading a charge over the rocks and scrub of Attica armed only with a telescope.

For the complete lack of any naval operations, other than those of Hastings in the *Kartería*, Cochrane blamed only the Greeks. His comments on the men under his nominal command were merciless:

"It was impossible to induce the Greek seamen to submit to the slightest restraint on their inclinations, or to render the most trifling service without being paid in advance, or to perform such service after being so paid, if it suited their interest or convenience to evade the fulfilment of their engagement. More than six crews have passed under my review on board the *Hellas* in the course of as many months, exclusive of those in other vessels, and notwithstanding all that has been written to praise the courage of the Greek seamen they are collectively the greatest cowards I have ever met with."

The Greeks had very little more use for Cochrane than he had for them. Their distinguished historian, Spyridon Trikoupis—a passionate Anglophile who later served as Greek Minister in London—wrote that[1] "never had the Greeks suffered such a disaster or one of such magnitude" as was brought upon them by Cochrane's "frenzy" (*paraphorá*). Such was his verdict on Cochrane's attempt to relieve the siege of Athens.

British accounts, especially George Finlay's, go far to confirm Trikoupis' severe judgement. Cochrane's fatal arrogance led him to insist on commanding operations not only at sea but on land, in spite of the simultaneous arrival of Sir Richard Church. Church was much more familiar with the Greeks, who adored him. "Our father is at last come," was Kolokotronis' welcome to him: "We have only to obey him and our liberty is secured." Church should have resisted Cochrane's pretensions to enlarge his command, but was too courteous and conciliatory to do so. His principal service at this time was to reconcile the warring factions of the Greeks, whom Cochrane was

[1] Trikoupis, *Istoría tís Ellinikís Epanastáseos* (London, 1853–57), vol. IV, p. 119.

too impatient to understand. It would have been better if Church had applied his undoubted abilities to organising the relief of Athens, which Cochrane's erratic enthusiasm did nothing to help. From every point of view, it was as important to save the Acropolis in 1827 as it had been to save Mesolonghi in 1824. All the weight of philhellenism was available to concentrate upon the task – Gordon, Hastings, Finlay, the Urquhart brothers, and a dozen others, as well as Church and Cochrane and the surviving Greek commanders, Miaoulis in the *Hellas* and Karaiskakis on land. But in Finlay's terse phrase,[1] "there was little community of views between the Lord High Admiral and the generalissimo". Church yielded, and thanks to Cochrane's impatience, the opportunity was botched and thrown away.

This is not the place to repeat the story[2] of the ill-contrived operations on sea and land which led to the surrender of the Acropolis to the Turks on 5th June, 1827. The effect of this disastrous and unnecessary setback was to reduce the Greeks to the brink of final defeat, and many of the philhellenes to despair. Cochrane sailed away contemptuously indifferent to the catastrophe he had precipitated. He wanted only to repeat the brilliant exploits which had won him fame in South America, but could not see how to do it. The result was aimless floundering. He set off for western Greece in the *Hellas*, his flagship, accompanied by Hastings in the *Kartería*, with no clear object in mind. There he left Hastings, who was completely disgusted with his commander-in-chief, and sailed for Alexandria to singe the Viceroy of Egypt's beard. The expedition was a fiasco. On his own admission, "nothing very material has been done by us", though it exasperated Admiral Codrington in command of the British Mediterranean fleet, who was hoping to bring about an armistice. A few further pinpricks at outlying points of Turkish power were all that Cochrane contributed to the struggle. He sailed

[1] Finlay, vol. VI, p. 426.

[2] A detailed account is in Dakin, *British and American Philhellenes*, pp. 149–158, with full references to first-hand stories by Cochrane, Gordon, Finlay and Greek participants, such as Makriyannis. The latter's account is translated in H. A. Lidderdale, *The Memoirs of General Makriyannis 1797–1864*, (London, 1966), pp. 123–42.

away early in 1828, returned later in the year to provoke fresh antagonisms, and left for good in November.

Meanwhile the true philhellenes, particularly Church and Hastings were making heroic efforts to rususcitate the flame of Greek resistance in the late summer of 1827. Church rallied what forces he could, and marched across the northern Peloponnese with the intention of crossing the Gulf of Corinth to stir a fresh rebellion in Akarnania. Hastings with the *Kartería*, – the most modern fighting-ship in the Mediterranean, equipped not only with steam-power but with his own invention for firing red-hot shot – remained in the Gulf of Corinth, partly to cover Church's movements and partly to watch the powerful fleet assembled under Ibrahim Pasha in the Bay of Navarino. That fleet was also the target for Admiral Codrington with a much weaker squadron of the Royal Navy. Admiral de Rigny, commanding the Levant Station of the French Navy, also had Ibrahim under observation; and before long a Russian fleet under the ex-Dutch Admiral Heiden was to converge on the same target. All these forces were brought together by the Treaty of London in July 1827, which was designed, though not very clearly or skilfully, to bring about an armistice in the war. Whether the Treaty by itself could have achieved its object may be doubted. The issue was forced, however, by the activities of the philhellenes, particularly Hastings; to a lesser extent by the movements of Church, and even in a remoter sense by the irresponsible antics of Cochrane.

The Treaty and the instructions based on it required the three allied Admirals to enforce an armistice on the Greeks and Turks without becoming involved in hostilities. Although the Greeks accepted the armistice in principle, Church, Hastings and Cochrane all ignored it in practice. Consequently Ibrahim Pasha ignored it also. Apart from mercilessly ravaging the Peloponnese, he was also determined to chastise Hastings for a particularly brilliant exploit in the Bay of Salona (an inlet in the northern coast of the Gulf of Corinth) at the end of September, in which he destroyed seven Turkish ships. Ibrahim and his fleet set out from the Bay of Navarino to avenge this defeat, but Codrington forced him to turn back. He also required

Cochrane and Church to desist from operations, though neither was under his orders, both being servants of the Greek government. The intolerable tension of the situation finally led to Codrington's decision, supported by the French and Russian Admirals, to sail into the Bay of Navarino, where Ibrahim's larger but less efficient fleet lay at anchor. What precisely Codrington intended to happen has always been obscure. What actually happened was the battle of Navarino on 20th October, 1827, which ensured the independence of Greece by destroying the Turkish-Egyptian fleet, and incidentally precipitated a Russo-Turkish War.

Wellington called the battle an "untoward event", and others had harsher names for it. But the philhellenes were naturally jubilant. Even Cochrane wrote warmly to Church: "*Now* therefore is the moment for the Greeks to act and for you to cover yourself with glory"; though he did not omit to add a request for funds, "for I have not a dollar to pay the men with". Church in his turn responded with the enthusiasm that might be expected of him. In a circular letter to all the Greek commanders, he wrote:[1]

"The tremendous roar of the artillery of hundreds of ships of war, and the continual lightning of consuming fire, blazing awfully to announce the repeated peals bursting like thunder from thousands of heavy cannon will have already announced to many the glorious event of the destruction of the Turko-Egyptian fleet in the harbour of Navarino by the allied fleet of England, France and Russia under the supreme direction of His Exy Admiral Sir E. Codrington, and his noble supporters Admirals de Rigny and de Heyden—To those who from distance from the shores of Navarin could not have had the extreme delight of hearing the thunder of the Battle I have now the pleasure to communicate this signal interposition of divine Providence by the chastizing hands of the three Christian powers in favour of Greece in favour of the Hellenic race. I need say no more I think to tell you to redouble your efforts in the service of your Country—Ibrahim Pasha who makes war even on your fruit trees and who avoids the serious and bloody combat with men, to make

[1] Crawley, pp. 232–3.

slaves of your helpless children of both sexes for brutal purposes—whose most sacred and most secret asylums are assail'd by his ferocious bands whilst he keeps aloof from manly warfare—this Pasha this ferocious Pasha now contemplates with dismay the remains and wrecks of that late mighty Turko-Egyptian fleet which had brought so many thousand Turks and Arabs to your shores and which had so amply provided them with all their wants—It is with a truly joyful heart that I communicate to you this great event, and desire you to make it known—to all the troops and inhabitants in your vicinity. I salute you.

RICHARD CHURCH, Generalissimo."

There were many tribulations to come, but for the moment philhellenism could be satisfied. In Victor Hugo's words,

La Grèce est libre et dans la tombe
Byron applaudit Navarin.

CHAPTER VI

The Aftermath

For most of the philhellenes, though not all, the battle of Navarino marked the end of the road. There is a long list of recorded names of whom little is known and no more is heard.[1] Many had fallen by the wayside: Humphreys, Fenton, Lord Charles Murray and others, as well as Byron. Frederick North, Earl of Guilford, the most lovable and sincere of all the philhellenes, though never a combatant, died barely a week before Navarino. Some had fallen and others were still to fall in the closing stages of the campaign: Whitcombe redeeming his sorry reputation in the battle for Athens, Scanlan in Hastings' brilliant victory off Salona, Kirkman Finlay and Charles Urquhart early in 1828. Others to whom the Greek war of independence was only a passing phase in a career to be pursued elsewhere had already left the scene: Stanhope to inherit an earldom; Emerson to become a distinguished civil servant as Sir James Emerson Tennent; Bulwer to win eccentric fame as a diplomatist; Gordon (who later returned) to write his superlative *History of the Greek Revolution*; Trelawny to live to a ripe old age of buccaneering and braggadocio; Parry to drink himself to death; Blaquière to return to the sea, where he was drowned a few years later.

That the heroic days were over was marked by a series of deflationary events in 1828. Capodistrias arrived to assume the role of *Kyvernítis* (Governor or President) at the end of January. Almost on the same day the Speech from the Throne at the opening of Parliament in London apologised for the "untoward event" of the battle of Navarino. In August Codrington was recalled from his

[1] More than thirty, apart from the better-known names, are recorded in the index to Dakin, *British and American Philhellenes*. See Appendix I, pp. 179–81.

command in the Mediterranean for having misinterpreted his instructions—not specifically for having been at fault in joining battle at Navarino, though he was held to blame for having inadvertently set in motion a train of events which led to the outbreak of war between Russia and Turkey. A few weeks later a French army was landed in the Peloponnese to compel the withdrawal of Ibrahim Pasha, who was willing enough to depart provided that a show of force was mounted to save his face. Meanwhile—most fatal sign of all in the eyes of those who had devoted themselves as freelance heroes to the cause—the diplomatists were beginning to arrive: a French Resident in June, a Russian in September, a British Resident in November. Though they did not see eye to eye with each other or with Capodistrias, all agreed in wishing to be rid of the philhellenes and their supporting banditry. As Capodistrias once put it with incautious frankness, "il faut éteindre les brandons de la révolution".

Capodistrias' relations with the philhellenes were particularly ambiguous. He was a diplomatist and an administrator, devoted to orderly procedures and well versed in international negotiation. He had reasons both to approve and to disapprove of the philhellenes, and the reasons varied in different cases. First, there were reasons of nationality. Most of the philhellenes were British, and the British were in occupation of his native islands; on the other hand, he needed the support of Britain's naval and financial strength to consolidate his country's independence. There were virtually no Russian philhellenes, but he also needed the support of Russia as the one Orthodox great power; there were a number of French and Bavarian philhellenes, and both the French and Bavarian governments were trying to establish a strong position in the new state; and there were a few Swiss and Americans, whom he probably liked best because their countries were republics, remote from Greece and disinterested in power politics. But inevitably he depended most on the British, because they were the most firmly entrenched. Church and Hastings in particular were in command of the effective forces on land and sea.

As it happened, too, Capodistrias saw eye to eye with Church and

Hastings on what needed to be done to consolidate the infant state. The great powers were concerned to limit the size as well as the independence of Greece. Wellington in particular wished to deprive the Greeks both of the islands of the Aegean and also of mainland territory north of the Gulf of Corinth. He dreaded an independent Greece adjacent to the Ionian Islands, which the British government had decided to retain in an almost colonial state of dependence. The French and Russian governments had no such intimate interests, but were little disposed to enlarge the boundaries of the new state unless they could dominate it. Capodistrias, on the other hand, was determined both to enlarge his new homeland and to maintain its independence from all the great powers. In this task, though they disagreed on many other matters, he had the loyal support of Church and Hastings. Together with their brave *kapetánioi* on land and sea, they set out to rouse and conquer the north-west. Others at the same time sailed to capture the islands—Fabvier and Cochrane to Chios, Hane and Charles Urquhart to Crete.

The expeditions to the islands were a failure, which cost the philhellenes valuable lives: Kirkman Finlay in action off Chios, and Charles Urquhart in an accident on Graboussa, an islet off the coast of Crete, long notorious as a nest of pirates. But in the north-west it was another story. Capodistrias, Church and Hastings, though they often disagreed on tactics, all saw alike what needed to be done: they must seize and hold as much territory as possible north of the Gulf of Corinth. Navpaktos (Lepanto), Mesolonghi and the forts held by the Turks northwards as far as Arta must be captured. At the same time Greek forces under Dimitrios Ypsilantis were to push northwards from the Isthmus of Corinth, to recover the strongholds lost to the Turks in Attica and Boeotia, including particularly Athens. In the Peloponnese itself a show of force by the French troops was sufficient to secure the surrender by the Turks of all the forts they still held: Patras, Navarino, Modon and Coron were all in Greek hands by the autumn of 1828. But the French commander was forbidden to support the Greeks' campaigns outside the Peloponnese.

While the fate of Greece was still imperfectly decided, one

symptom of normality was already apparent again. The tourists were back: the scholars, the clergymen, the antiquarians, the romantics, the officers on leave, the diplomatists and the rest. Indeed, they had never been wholly absent. The Rev. Charles Swan, chaplain to the Embassy at Constantinople, had recorded a visit in 1824–25, "including many interesting particulars relative to the Greek Revolution, especially a journey through Maina to the camp of Ibrahim Pasha, together with observations on the antiquities, opinions, and usages of Greece as they now exist". Here, in fact, was everything in a nutshell. The same ground was covered by R. R. Madden in the years 1824–27; by John Carne in 1826; and by Captain Charles Colville Frankland in 1827–28. An even more ambitious range was comprehended by the Rev. R. Walsh in *A Residence at Constantinople*, "during a period including the commencement, progress, and termination of the Greek and Turkish revolutions". The only comment called for by their tedious reminiscences is that none was any more touched by true philhellenism than their pre-Byronic predecessors, The struggle for independence, still only on the brink of final success. continued almost unnoticed by the returning tourists.

The operations of Church and Hastings were the most important events of these years, because the area where they took place was the most doubtful of all Capodistrias' claims to Greek sovereignty. Judged by results, they were successful, but not without friction, frustration and tragedy. The most tragic event was the death of Hastings from a severe wound suffered in a combined attack on Anatoliko, the fort guarding Mesolonghi. After Byron, he was the greatest loss of all to the Greeks. Although haughty and domineering, and as resentful of discipline himself as he was ruthless in imposing it on others, he was by common consent the bravest and most skilful of all the combatant philhellenes. By comparison, Cochrane was irresponsible and Church over-cautious. George Finlay, who had a good right to judge, classed Hastings as the best of the philhellenes,[1] and called him "as distinguished for sincerity and truth in private life, as for ability and daring in war". Gordon and Trikoupis confirmed

[1] Finlay, vol. VI, p. 397; vol. VII, pp. 24–5.

Finlay's opinion in their histories. It was unfortunate that the one man with whom he could seldom agree was Church, who had to be his closest collaborator in the last days of his life.

Church nevertheless paid generous tribute to Hastings and continued the operations which they had planned together. He took Vonitsa on the Gulf of Arta in March 1829, thus enabling his forces to outflank the Turks' mainland forts. In April Navpaktos surrendered, though Capodistrias' useless brother Agostino arrived at the eleventh hour to usurp the honour of receiving the surrender; and in May Church took Mesolonghi in a combined operation, which he and Hastings had attempted unsuccessfully the previous year. Meanwhile the Greeks had also won their own successes under Dimitrios Ypsilantis: Salona (Amphissa) and Karpenisi fell to them before the end of 1828; Athens was blockaded, and Ypsilantis won the last battle of the war between Thebes and Levadia in September 1829. The armistice between Turkey and Russia a few weeks earlier, followed by the Treaty of Adrianople, which imposed humiliating terms on the Sultan, brought about the final settlement of the Greek War of Independence. Thanks to the astute diplomacy of Capodistrias, and the courage and skill of Church and Hastings, the new state of Greece was to be decidedly larger than the great powers had originally designed.

Still, all was not plain sailing, nor was the work of the philhellenes yet complete. Church unfortunately quarrelled with Capodistrias at the height of his success. Capodistrias found Church's troops undisciplined, and resented his prestige among the *kapetánioi*; Church complained that he never received supplies or pay for his men in time, and resented the interference of Agostino Capodistrias in his role as Lieutenant Plenipotentiary in northern Greece. An increasingly disagreeable correspondence between the President and his field commander, followed by an angry interview in June 1829 on the island of Aegina, culminated in an open quarrel. The painful scene was set in July at the National Assembly convened by Capodistrias at Argos to ratify his actions and policy. Although the President's prestige was at its height, there was much resentment among those who suffered from his arbitrary rule and his disregard of the constitution, which had been enacted before he took office. The constitutionalists were supported by Church, who arrived at Argos accompanied by Finlay and Gordon, with a letter of resignation in his pocket. Capodistrias and his entourage treated the British party with open contempt.

Church's letter was dignified and emotional. "I do not separate myself from Greece in heart," he declared, and went on:

"Those who have served their country under my immediate orders can bear witness to what I had daily to suffer—not from the Greek nation certainly, nor from the brave military who supported me, but from the system adopted by the Government, which was ill-calculated to aid our military operations, but well adapted to drive from his post any general who did not feel, as I did, that he had devoted his humble services not to the individual at the head of Government for the time, but to the Greek Nation."

Church tried to read out his letter to the National Assembly, but was shouted down by "that corrupt and illegally chosen body, which misrepresented rather than represented the Greek nation," as he described it. It gave Capodistrias an overwhelming vote of confidence; and Church left the country a few days later. Gordon and Finlay, however, both stayed on to await happier days.

But Greece had by no means seen or heard the last of Church. The great debate over Greece's boundaries continued, and he had a right to take part in it. While seeking a permanent sovereign for Greece, the great powers repeatedly pushed the lines on the map to and fro, balancing geographical extent against degrees of independence. In 1830 they persuaded Leopold of Saxe-Coburg to accept the crown, but only of a kingdom truncated of the area conquered in Church's last campaign. Capodistrias was disgusted, both by his own supersession and also by the loss of territory; and on the latter point, though not the former, Church was at one with him. Capodistrias forcefully pointed out to Leopold all the disadvantages of his future situation. Church lent reinforcement with a pamphlet in February 1830, entitled "Observations on an eligible line of frontier for Greece as an Independent State", criticising the proposed reduction of the frontier. The trick worked: Leopold renounced the crown,[1] and lived to become the first King of the Belgians a year later; but Capodistrias retained his presidency at a heavy cost, which he paid with his life in October 1831.

Church could not be held to blame for the assassination of Capodistrias, intimate though he was with the constitutionalists who inspired and condoned it; nor was he even in Greece at the time. Gordon was a little nearer to direct implication. The murder of Capodistrias was due to the convergence of many factors: his own uncompromising and authoritarian character, the resentment of the constitutionalists, and a personal quarrel with the family of Petrobey Mavromikhalis. The Mavromikhalis family, which held hereditary dominion over the tip of the Peloponnese known as the Mani or Maina, had no particular love for constitutions, but they resented Capodistrias' refusal to compensate them for their losses in the war. A series of plots against Capodistrias burgeoned in the course of 1831 from a multitude of causes, and there were serious risings against his government in the north, in the Peloponnese and in the islands, based on Ydra. Capodistrias was particularly concerned about the rebellious "Spartiates" as he called the Mavromikhalis family. Petrobey, the head of the clan, held an official position at Nauplia, the temporary capital, and Capodistrias was determined to keep him there, under his own surveillance. But in January 1831 Petrobey slipped away from Nauplia to Zante, on Gordon's private yacht. Later in the year he returned to the Peloponnese, was arrested, and held in confinement again at Nauplia.

Gordon played no known part in the risings which followed, culminating in the murder of Capodistrias on 9th October by one of Petrobey's sons. There followed a state of anarchy lasting more than a year. The remaining philhellenes were aghast at the bloody aftermath to their efforts on behalf of Greece, which appeared likely to end in chaos and anarchy. Some did indeed conclude that they had

[1] His resignation was drafted for him by the Earl of Durham, who as John Lambton had been an original member of the London Greek Committee (Dakin, p. 198).

been wasting their time liberating the Greeks. The case of Dr. Millingen, who went over to the Turks and entered the service of the Sultan's court, is an early example of such disillusionment, though his motives were in large part mercenary. A more significant case is that of David Urquhart, a sincere and courageous Scot whose motives none could impugn. He had fought in a number of actions, including the battle of Salona Bay under Hastings; and after the fighting was over, his philhellenism was converted into the administration of relief with Dr. Howe and other Americans. But in May 1830 he set off on a tour to the north, through the territory recently conquered by Church and across the still undemarcated frontier into Turkey. What he found there turned him from a philhellene into a passionate Turcophil.

Originally he had shared all the sentimentality of the educated British about Greece. In his remarkable book, *Spirit of the East*, he confesses to the familiar prejudices based on the classics and antiquities of Greece. He quotes Herodotus, Thucydides, Polybius, Strabo; he depicts a Homeric feast ("not a representation, but a real scene, from the wars of Troy"); he meditates in the vale of Tempe and enthuses over Greek mythology; he rejoices in Suliote hospitality and the brigandage of Mount Olympus; and he tells a touchingly romantic story of Aglae, a Greek bride, and the bandit to whom she was betrothed. He combines, in fact, the schoolboy enthusiasm which Byron mocked with the romantic realism which Byron pioneered. For good measure, he even makes a comparison between the Greeks and his fellow-countrymen, distinctly to the advantage of the Greeks. Describing a Greek *kapetánios*, he writes:[1]

"The style, the outline of the figure, the arms, the tail, suggested the comparison with the old Scottish chieftain; but the climate, the refinement of manner, the classical language, and I must, in spite of early associations, say elegance of costume, were in favour of the Greek. The struggles of the Scotch Highlanders and of the Greek mountaineers, probably, had very many points of resemblance, but their principles and results have been very dissimilar. The Scotch

[1] Urquhart, vol. I, p. 128.

bravely shed their blood for the sinking cause of bigotry; the Greeks for that of rising liberty; and fortunately, the same principle triumphed in the failure of the former and the success of the latter."

But as his journey progressed, he found himself more and more disenchanted with the Greeks and impressed by the Turks. He describes the transference of his emotions from one side to the other in an eloquent passage which begins with a comparison of the Greek and Turkish flags:[1]

"Compare this pale and chequered standard with the gorgeous colours of the Ottoman; bold, rich and simple—the day star of fortune, and the crescent of power, emblazoned on a purple cloud. Most poetic among standards! Most spirit-stirring among national emblems! And how much of the enthusiasm that stirs the spirit, and nerves the arm, may not depend on the poetry of an emblem? Could a nation—could even a faction exist without the rhetoric of colour? What, then, must not be the effect of clothing the personification of nationality with beauty, and of inspiring its martial genius by associating with its glory the sublimest works of nature? All these are united in the standard of the Ottomans, and are combined in no other. This, too, is the historic standard, which has flown, with the swiftness of a thunder-cloud, over Asia, Europe, and Africa, from the palaces of Delhi to the foot of Atlas; from the wastes of Abyssinia to the marshes of the Don; which has proved its power on the plains of Tours and Roncesvalles, before the walls of Vienna, on the Indus and the Oxus. Thirty years after its birth, it had humbled the two greatest empires of that day; and, in eighty years, boasted more tributary lands than Rome had subdued in eight centuries. That flag had now disappeared from the castles, where I saw it so lately, reddened at once with anger and with shame; and, as the Scythians of old rehearsed before the departed the history of their lives, so now did I dwell on the features and the story of that personification of Mussulman greatness which had sunk before my eyes, while I marvelled at the means by which it had been overthrown."

This is the prose of a spiritual dreamer meditating on symbols.

[1] Urquhart, vol. I, pp. 36–7.

But the symbols had for Urquhart a deep foundation of reality derived from his own experience and observation. The same passage continues thus:

"When I first landed on the shores of Greece, more interested in the nature of the rocks than in the sanguinary contest which was there proceeding, I was soon filled with hatred and aversion for the Turkish name; and, with the enthusiasm of youthful feeling, I became a partisan. But the Ottoman, who had aroused this animosity by the violence of triumph, dispelled it when he appeared in defeat and captivity – a personification of stoical firmness and of dignified resignation. The sympathy which is the tribute of misfortune, I now transferred to the vanquished; but that sympathy was combined with admiration for a fortitude and respect for a character, the energy and durability of which I never could have known but for the trial to which I had seen it subjected."

These paragraphs come early in a long and profound study of the two peoples whose history has been so closely intertwined since the 14th century. It is full of detailed, soberly documented, factual information, never wantonly disparaging the Greeks for whom Urquhart had nearly sacrificed his life, but always giving the Turks the better of the argument. He ended by believing that he had been personally guilty of a grave crime in helping to disrupt the Ottoman Empire.

Two quotations may sum up Urquhart's considered attitude towards the two peoples.[1] The Greeks, he writes, "coiled themselves round the heart of the Ottoman Empire" and "corrupted the simplicity of the Turkish system by their political doctrines, the primitiveness of the Turkish pastoral habits by the servility of their own bearing and conduct". On the other hand, "the legitimate principles of the internal administration of Turkey are such, that no set of men could ever be the objects of public sympathy by the infraction of them". The force and cogency with which these conclusions are buttressed in Urquhart's masterpiece are important, because he strongly influenced public opinion in Britain, up to and

[1] Urquhart, vol. I, pp. 88 and 195.

beyond the Crimean War. Nor was he alone in propagating Turkish sympathies. Hostility to the Greeks had already found a sharp voice in P. J. Green, formerly Consul at Patras, whose *Sketches of the War in Greece* appeared in 1827. Even so devoted a philhellene as George Finlay also helped by the sardonic bitterness with which he commented on the results of the War of Independence in retrospect.[1]

Even during the war, volunteers from the west had not been confined to the Greek forces. French officers were particularly active on the side of the enemy. Napoleon's officers reorganised the Turkish army as well as the Greek irregulars; Colonel Sève, who had founded a military school at Assouan, accompanied Ibrahim Pasha in the Peloponnese; Captain Letellier helped to create the Egyptian fleet; and he and other French officers managed the disposition of Ibrahim Pasha's ships in the bay of Navarino in October 1827. There was also at least one Englishman in Ibrahim's fleet, and a Colonel Romey in his forces on land.[2] Most of the British naval officers in the Mediterranean, as Captain Hamilton recorded, were more sympathetic to the Turks than to the Greeks.[3] The case of Dr. Millingen is also notorious; and an American Turcophil, George B. English, is also on record as having given up the Church to join the U.S. Marines, and thence gravitated to the Egyptian Army, in which he became a General.[4] These shifting sympathies need cause no surprise. The Turks had a good name in the west, especially after Russia emerged as a great power. Philhellenes were always a minority: public opinion in general accepted the view summed up in a later slogan, that "Johnny Turk was a gentleman."

Others who had played no part in the war contributed to the same propaganda. Disraeli, for instance, despite his admiration for Byron, despised the Greeks and never ceased to praise the Turks from the time of his first encounter with them in 1830. He visited the Peloponnese, Athens and Ioannina, where his arrival almost coincided

[1] Finlay, vol. VI, p. 198.
[2] Finlay, vol. VI, pp. 353n., 360.
[3] See p. 64 above.
[4] Larrabee, p. 45.

with that of Urquhart, shortly after the governor had crushed an Albanian revolt.[1] To his sister Disraeli wrote:

"I find the habits of this calm and luxurious people entirely agree with my own preconceived opinions of propriety and enjoyment, and I detest the Greeks more than ever."

These sentiments remained strong within him throughout his political career: they account for the bitter attack by the philhellene historian, Edward Freeman, on "the Jew in his drunken insolence". They were welcome, however, to the British ruling class, which was in an anti-Russian mood and subjected to continual irritation at the hands of the Greeks during the early decades of independence.

There were still voices on the other side, of course. While the negotiations over Greece's boundaries were going on in 1828–29, Aberdeen—Byron's "Athenian Aberdeen", who was now Foreign Secretary—sent private advice to Capodistrias to stand firm in his insistence on extended frontiers. Stratford Canning, who had been a friend of Sir Richard Church for many years and a colleague of Capodistrias in Switzerland in 1814, gave open encouragement to the Greeks while on his way to Constantinople as Ambassador for the first time. Palmerston, then a junior minister at the War Office, protested at the evident absurdity of excluding from Greece's frontiers the historic towns of Athens, Thebes, Marathon, Salamis, Plataea, Thermopylae, and Mesolonghi. (He was to take a different line towards the Greeks during the dispute over the claims of Don Pacifico in 1850, when he sent the Royal Navy to blockade Piraeus.) The arguments Palmerston invoked from ancient history were typical of fashionable philhellenism. And to show that the sentiment was not dead in a later generation, Gladstone, then a schoolboy at Eton, appeared at the ceremony of Montem wearing the "petticoats of a Greek mountaineer". He too was later to find his philhellenism wearing thin, when he was appointed High Commissioner Extraordinary to the Ionian Islands in 1858; and he then decided that it would be "nothing less than a crime against the safety of Europe" to cede them to Greece. But that "crime" was

[1] Blake, *Disraeli*, pp. 52, 64, 579.

duly committed in 1863, with Gladstone's assent. So long as the British ruling class was brought up on the classics, sentiment could cover a multitude of sins.

The main charge against the Greeks in the early days of independence was their incapacity to govern themselves. This was the reason put forward by A. W. Kinglake in *Eothen* for the fact that the Greeks remaining under Turkish rule were more contented than their nominally independent brethren. The British public had, or thought it had, plenty of grounds to support such criticism. There were recurrent outbreaks of brigandage on the northern frontiers, some of which were brought under control by Church and Gordon in their capacity as Generals of the Greek Army. Their success in influencing the brigands, who had served under them in the war of independence, confirmed both Church and Gordon in their philhellenism. Others had unhappier experiences. When the scholarly tourists returned to Greece, one of the most eminent among them was the Rev. Christopher Wordsworth, nephew of the poet and a future Headmaster of Harrow and Bishop of Lincoln. With another learned companion, he was attacked and nearly captured by bandits in 1833. Urquhart was actually captured by Greek bandits, though not on Greek soil, and he mightily enjoyed the experience. A generation later in 1870 a more spectacular and tragic case of brigandage ended in the murder of a group of English tourists near Marathon.

To blame the Greek people for these crimes was not wholly just, for during the early decades of independence they were not in control of their own destiny. A Bavarian monarchy supported by Bavarian troops was imposed on them, so that the blame for disorders lay largely on foreigners, whose court was sometimes suspected of being in league with the brigands. The remaining philhellenes appreciated this fact, even if the British government did not. Edward Masson, for example, the Scottish schoolmaster who settled permanently in Greece, qualified as a lawyer and loyally served the new state both as a judge and Attorney-General; but he did not hesitate to enter into dispute with the new authorities when he thought it right to do so. He could argue a point of law with Capodistrias, and even defended his assassin, George Mavromikhalis. Later he prosecuted Kolokotronis for conspiracy, but later still he was suspected of being involved in a conspiracy to impose a constitution on the Bavarian monarchy. So was Gordon, who was relieved of his command. Finlay also had no reason to love the Bavarians, who confiscated part of his property near Athens in 1840 in order to build a country house for King Otho, as Otto of Bavaria was known in Greece.

Almost all the philhellenes who remained in Greece sided with the constitutionalists in their many disputes with the absolutism of the Bavarian regency and monarchy. They sympathised with the various plots to introduce a constitution, and in some cases were actually implicated in them. Gordon fell out with King Otho, and resigned his Greek commission in 1839. Hane, who had been made a Colonel in the Greek army, was dismissed from employment for the same reason in 1842. Finlay was described by Otho as "a violent liberal and active constitutionalist and therefore dangerous", though he did little more than publish critical and sardonic articles in *The Times*. Church was deeply involved with his former comrades-in-arms in the conspiracy of September 1843, which forced the King to accept a constitution; but it was mainly thanks to his moderating influence that Otho did not lose his throne on that occasion. Nevertheless, King Otho ungratefully dismissed Church from his post as Inspector-General of the Greek Army, only to recall him ten years later at the time of the Crimean War. It was no surprise to any of the philhellenes when the King lost his throne in 1862.

By that time, all the transient philhellenes of an earlier generation had moved to other careers or conflicts elsewhere. Cochrane had succeeded to the earldom of Dundonald in 1831 and secured his reinstatement in the Royal Navy as a Rear-Admiral in the following year. As late as 1848 he was appointed Commander-in-Chief of the West Indies and North American Station, but he was never employed again, though he lived till 1860. Codrington also never saw the like of his Mediterranean command again. He lived till 1851, devoting his last twenty years to seeking justice for his officers and men, who had been denied compensation for their losses at Navarino because "hostile proceedings were not contemplated in the instructions." Only by entering Parliament in 1831 and campaigning in the House of Commons did he finally secure justice in 1834. But although he was appointed Commander-in-Chief at Portsmouth in 1839, his career, like Cochrane's, was already effectively at an end. Not so with Napier, who became a successful Commander-in-Chief in India, where he took John Pitt Kennedy (the Sinner) with him as his Military Secretary. His sympathy with radical causes lasted till the end, and he always hoped to be appointed High Commissioner in the Ionian Islands.

A decade after his service in the Ionian Islands, and before his great days in India, Napier found himself required in 1839 to take measures against the Chartists as Commander of the Northern District in England. His sympathies, however, were with the Chartists, for the same reasons as they had been with the Ionian Greeks.[1] So were those of others who had shared in the struggle for Greek independence, such as David Urquhart and Joseph Hume. Others had mellowed into figures of the Establishment: some minor, like Leicester Stanhope, the fifth Earl of Harrington, or Sir Henry Lytton Bulwer, first and only Lord Dalling and Bulwer; some major, like Lord John Russell, who as Foreign Secretary in 1862 presided over the cession of the Ionian Islands to Greece, the very thought of which Gladstone had declared a year earlier to be "a crime against the peace of Europe". It has to be admitted that the flame of philhellenism burned low in the thirty years of King Otho's troubled reign, chiefly because the cause of the Greeks was so intimately associated with Russian imperialism. Palmerston's blockade of the Piraeus in 1850 for the benefit of Don Pacifico and George Finlay, and the repetition of it under Aberdeen, Russell and Palmerston from 1854 to 1857 in support of the Crimean War, demonstrated clearly that devotion to a classical education was not enough.

Meanwhile, few of the British philhellenes still survived in Greece.

[1] Briggs, *The Age of Improvement*, p. 309.

Six are know to have made their homes permanently there: Gordon, Finlay, Masson, Church, Fitz-Gibbon, Hane; and it is striking that three of them were Scots and one (or possibly two) Irish by birth. All were devoted to Greece, even under governments which they detested. All had left Greece at one time or another, and inevitably returned. Each of them might have said in the words of the modern Greek poet, George Sepheris: "However far I go voyaging, still Greece wounds me". Apart from Fitz-Gibbon and Hane, of whose later years little is known, all left written records. Church's papers in the British Museum are only incompletely published, though they have been substantially used by later writers.[1] Masson published *Philhellenika* in 1852, containing translations of Greek ballads, a preface on philhellenism, and a poem of his own. Gordon and Finlay were both considerable historians of the Greek revolution, and the latter also of the whole span of Greek history from the Roman conquest to his own day.

Unhappily, being all experts in Greek affairs, the philhellenes continued to disagree with each other as well as with the Greek authorities. The British government, which became increasingly entangled in Greek politics under Palmerston and Gladstone, was regaled with contradictory and dogmatic advice from Church and Finlay in particular. But Church and Finlay, both of whom survived into the 1870s, had different ideas about what was good for the Greeks. Their differences were sharpened by personal animosity after Finlay published his *History of the Greek Revolution* in 1861, with its severe and unfair criticisms of Church. Although the two men had been friends for many years, and Finlay had earlier paid tribute to Church as "the liege lord of all the true Philhellenes", he omitted Church's name altogether from his list of the most distinguished participants in the War of Independence. He belittled Church's campaign in the north-west, which had in fact ensured the extension of Greece's boundaries to include Aitolo-Akarnania, and

[1] Notably by E. M. Church, *Sir Richard Church in Italy and Greece* (Edinburgh, 1895); C. W. Crawley, *The Question of Greek Independence, 1821–33* (Cambridge, 1930); and Douglas Dakin, *British and American Philhellenes* (Thessaloniki, 1955).

declared[1] that "as a military man, his career in Greece was a signal failure". Of his policy over the disbandment of the irregulars after the war, Finlay concluded[2] that "Sir Richard Church committed the political blunder of joining the cause of the anarchists". Church was bitterly hurt by these criticisms, of which he had no forewarning, and a sarcastic and insulting correspondence ensued.

The breach was never healed in Church's lifetime. No doubt it contributed to the opposing positions which the two men took on subsequent events in the troubled affairs of Greece. When King Otho was deposed in 1862, for instance, Church supported the popular clamour of the Greeks that he should be succeeded by Queen Victoria's second son, Prince Alfred. Finlay, on the other hand, proposed that Greece should become a republic, with Gladstone himself as President. This was an interesting reversion to the view fashionable among many of the early philhellenes, such as Stanhope, under the influence of Bentham. Another of the former Benthamites, Henry Lytton Bulwer, now Ambassador at Constantinople, had yet another idea. He proposed through Greek friends in Constantinople that a Regency should be established in Greece, and that he himself should be Regent. None of them in the end had his way. The great powers preferred a Danish prince, who became King George I and reigned for almost half a century. The philhellenes in the end accepted that this was a satisfactory arrangement, given the character of the Greek nation, though they might not have been wholly surprised if they could have foreseen the later history of the new dynasty.

Both the two old philhellenes surviving in Athens mellowed in their old age: Finlay less so than Church, who always had a more equable temperament. Church's last years were spent in dignified but almost penurious circumstances, surrounded by admiring friends of all ages: old *kapetánioi*, senators, politicians, university professors, islanders, courtiers, provincial governors, diplomatists, men who remembered Byron and youths to whom he was an immortal name. Church delivered of himself a splendid epitaph:

[1] Finlay, vol. VI, p. 418.
[2] Finlay, vol. VII, p. 118.

"I do not regret having sacrificed everything to the cause I embraced, and to whose triumph I hope I contributed."

When he died in 1873, in his ninetieth year, all Greece mourned him as a great hero, and even Finlay made amends: "There could not be a nobler heart, and I think he was a perfect model of what he considered a perfect knight". It is perhaps only an accident that the last words hint at a hidden qualification.

Finlay had indeed a sharp pen, with which he stabbed almost everyone involved in the War of Independence, except Byron and Hastings and a few of the nobler *kapetánioi* like Makriyannis. Byron told him in 1823 that he was "young and enthusiastic and therefore sure to be disappointed", which was a true prediction. He reflected bitterly on his disappointments in later years with unsparing objectivity. "When I had wasted as much money as I possessed, I turned my attention to study", he wrote of his great labours in the field of Greek history. It was true that he had failed in trying to run a model farm near Athens. Nor did he find writing history any more lucrative. "In a pecuniary point of view", he later wrote that he had "found cultivating the soil of Greece even more unprofitable than writing its history". Like all the British participants in the affairs of Greece during the revolution, apart from Lord Cochrane and a few members of the London Greek Committee, he ended up a poorer man than when he started. He died in 1875, criticising the Greeks to the last but fiercely attacking anyone else who dared to criticise them.

Meanwhile philhellenism had almost ceased to have meaning. The generation in whom it roused great expectations, whether liberal, romantic or mercenary, had passed away. The London Greek Committee passed into inglorious oblivion, though never formally dissolved. Its members turned their energies in new directions: Catholic emancipation had still to be achieved (1828); so had parliamentary reform (1832), the abolition of slavery (1834) and other progressive causes, to which members of the Committee were variously dedicated. On the other hand, those who had been induced by the Committee to subscribe to their loans had reason to wish they had stuck to one good cause at a time. Nor did philhellenic sentiment lead any members of the Committee to visit the land they had indirectly helped to liberate. Even of those who had been sent out during the war, none returned, so far as is known, with the single exception of George Cochrane, the Admiral's nephew, who tried to establish a steamship line in Greece in 1834. Though his venture was unsuccessful, it led him to write *Wanderings in Greece*, an agreeable work in a familiar vein, published in 1837.

For the most part, however, Grecian travel had slipped back into the pre-Byronic rut. The tourists began to flock back, as soon as it was more or less safe, though some of them met with alarming experiences. The British still predominated among them, though Frenchmen and Germans were also numerous, Americans and Swiss becoming more so, and even Russian, Dutch and Scandinavian travellers were beginning to offer their reminiscences to a discriminating public. Constantinople and the Turkish provinces were more popular than independent Greece, because there the traveller could combine antiquarianism with greater security. But the new kingdom also had an irresistible attraction. The scholars, the artists, the aristocrats, the soldiers and sailors, the elegant ladies with nothing else to do except paint water-colours, the Hellenic travellers, the romantics, all descended on Greece in rising quantities. Conducted tours began, and John Murray, Byron's publisher, brought out the first guide-book to Greece.[1] It warned the traveller against the piratical character of the Mainotes, the love of money which was the prevailing passion of the Greeks, and the absurd dogmas and superstitions of their church. It also advised him to take with him plenty of tea, porter and biscuits, and also "prints of the Queen, Ministers etc." to present to British consular agents, "who generally are natives".

It was as if Byron had never been. Most of the new generation of tourists scarcely deserve mention, and some of their publications are repulsive beyond words: for example, *Romaic Beauties and Trojan Humbugs*, by "Rattlebrain", or *Charley Chalk—the Career of an Artist*, by Jacob Parallel. Others are simply characteristic of their age

[1] *A Handbook for Travellers in the Ionian Islands, Greece, Turkey, Asia Minor and Constantinople* (London, 1840), pp. v-ix, 13, 22–3.

in a pathetically unmemorable way, like *Wayfaring Sketches among the Greeks and Turks*, by Felicia M. F. Skene (1847), or *Sunshine and Storm in the East*, by Mrs. Annie Brassey (1880). Titles abound among the new generation of travellers: the Marquess of Londonderry, the Earl of Carnarvon, Viscountess Strangford, the Earl of Carlisle, all honoured Greece with their presence and recorded their shallow experiences in conventional prose. More interesting than any of them was the Duchesse de Plaisance, an American in the same tradition as Lady Hester Stanhope though less aristocratic in her own right; but she unfortunately left no record of her eventful sojourn. A few, particularly the artists like Francis Hervé and Edward Lear, had something interesting to say. So had the great scholar, Christopher Wordsworth. He was the first Englishman to be presented to King Otho after his accession in 1833; he could boast first-hand experience of Greek brigandage; and his *Athens and Attica* (1837) was a notable landmark of scholarship. Others that may be set beside it in other areas of Hellenism were Robert Pashley's *Travels in Crete* (1837) and Robert Curzon's visits to the *Monasteries in the Levant* (1849).

For the rest, little need be said. Naval and army officers on leave hurried into print, but none came anywhere near the incomparable Colonel Leake. Clergymen did their bit, still persisting in the delusion that the Greeks could be won to protestantism: the Rev. John Hartley was at work on this forlorn mission before the war was over, and published his *Researches in Greece and the Levant* in 1831, which might be thought (but was not) to lay the matter to rest for ever. Journalists like W. M. Thackeray (who wrote his *Notes of a Journey from Cornhill to Cairo* under the pseudonym of M. A. Titmarsh in 1846), and A. W. Kinglake and Nassau Senior raised the standard of first-hand observations to a new level, though nothing could suppress the trivial chit-chat of the casual tourists. They continued endlessly to patronise, to mock and to complain. As late as 1850, the echoes of half a century earlier could still be heard:[1] Greek schoolmasters still had the absurd delusion that the western pronunciation of their language was wrong, their clergy were still ignorant and

[1] Aubrey de Vere, *Picturesque Sketches of Greece and Turkey* (London, 1850), pp. 16 182–5

superstitious, and a travelling milord must still lament: "What a calamity to be introduced to the boundless regions of intellect and fantasy with a mountebank for a guide!"

Occasionally a visitor to Greece is interesting for what he was to become. Such a one was Disraeli in 1830, with his Byronic delight in the flamboyant and the brutal; though his natural sympathies lay on the opposite side from Byron's—as did sometimes Byron's own. Another was a romantic youth called Richard Monckton Milnes, full of ecstatic dreams which too easily faded. He travelled for a time with Christopher Wordsworth, a contemporary at Cambridge, but soon found his company tedious. "The rough travelling", he also found "amusing enough for two or three days, is rather boring in the long run". Here was a classic type of the eternal undergraduate whom Byron ridiculed. The verses in which he commemorated his experiences were also typical. In his "Lines Expressive of the State of Feeling Excited by the Consciousness of Being in a Classic Country", he mused:

Oh, blessed, blessed be the Eld,
Its echoes and its shades,—
The tone that from all time outswelled,
The light that never fades;—
The silver-pinioned memories,
The symbol and the tale,—
The soul-enchasèd melodies
Of merriment and bale.

It is sad to think that one who was later, as Lord Houghton, a discriminating patron of poets as well as a devout admirer of Byron, could write such rubbish.

Many such romantic youths roamed and dreamed through Greece in the later 19th century. Few seem to have learned anything from Byron, whom all professed to admire. The truth is that none were philhellenes in the Byronic sense. To be a philhellene as Byron interpreted it was not to meditate, to admire battered statues, or to study amended texts: it was to suffer and to act. It was to know the people as they lived, not as pale shadows of the past like the ghosts of Achilles and Agamemnon in the eleventh book of the *Odyssey*. It was to share their lives, to sleep in caves, to sail a *caique* through a Mediterranean storm, to travel for days in wet clothes and tattered boots and a flea-ridden *capote*. It was to roast a spitted lamb on a camp-fire, and drink *rakí* from a goat-skin, and hear a Homeric *kapetánios* improvising such a song as Makriyannis sang one night during the siege of the Acropolis:[1]

The Sun had set (ah, men of Greece, a Sunset for you!)
And the Moon was no more to be seen,
No more to be seen the clear Morning Star,
Nor the Star of Eve that shines in its place,
For these four held council, and spoke in secret,
The Sun spins round and tells them, spins round and says
"*Last night when I set I hid myself behind a little rock,*
And I heard the weeping of women, and the mourning of men
For those slain heroes lying in the field,
And all the earth soaked in their blood—
Poor souls all gone below in their country's cause".

Even Byron had only dimly sensed the depth of the experience to come when he was first in Greece as a budding poet in 1809–10. The experience, without the significance, is on record as early as the *Siege of Corinth* (1816), and it is specifically dated to the year 1810:

We forded the river, and clomb the high hill,
Never our steeds for a day stood still;
Whether we lay in the cave or the shed
Our sleep fell soft on the hardest bed:
Whether we couched in our rough capote,
On the rougher plank of our gliding boat,
Or stretched on the beach, or our saddles spread
As a pillow beneath the resting head,
Fresh we woke upon the morrow:

[1] *The Memoirs of General Makriyannis 1797–1864* (edited and translated by H. A. Lidderdale, London, 1966), p. 111.

All our thoughts and words had scope,
We had health, and we had hope,
Toil and travel, but no sorrow.

An infinity of sorrow had been added to his happy memories of toil and travel before he wrote his last lines in Mesolonghi in 1824:

Seek out—less often sought than found—
A soldier's grave, for thee the best;
Then look around, and choose thy ground,
And take thy rest.

Neither the pre-Byronic nor the post-Byronic romantics in Greece could ever share or fathom the sympathy which united Byron and Makriyannis, the peer and the peasant, in bitter experience and poetic feeling. For what was needed was not simply an experience but a purpose.

Makriyannis, as it happened, was a severe but just judge of the philhellenes. A warrior of great courage and the noblest character himself, he had no need to flatter, nor did he do so. Cochrane he regarded with contemptuous anger; he was not enthusiastic about either Church or Gordon; Hastings and Byron he never mentions in his *Memoirs*, and Finlay only once. But some years after the war, he commissioned an artist called Panayotis Zographos, as untutored as he was himself in literature, to prepare a series of twenty-four illustrations of episodes in the war. The twenty-fourth of the series was called a "Memorial to the Philhellenes", in which were recorded the names of 390 men of all nationalities who took part in the war.[1] Many of them are unidentifiable, but to some at least of the familiar names Makriyannis renders homage: Hamilton, Byron, Gordon, Codrington, Cochrane, Church, Finlay and Hastings. His editor has classified all these as English, as is customary among the Greeks, though the list includes three Scots and two Irishmen. Similarly classified as English are several other names, some unidentifiable, but at least one certainly Swiss and another Bavarian.

[1] Angelos G. Prokopiou, *Tó Eikosiéna stí laikí zographikí tou* (Athens, 1940), pp. 200–207. A Swiss source makes the total 421: Dakin, *British and American Philhellenes*, p. 1.

These were men who had for the time being renounced nationality. Paradoxically, although fighting for a nationalist cause, nationalism was an ideology of which they were still unconscious in themselves. The number of those who had not yet a nation-state to call their own is striking: they came from Poland, from Italy, from the principalities of Germany, and above all from Scotland and Ireland. The catalogue of these last two nationalities, when all are assembled, is truly remarkable. At least a dozen of each can be counted with certainty in or near the field, and among the known total of eighty-two British names there are probably many more of less identifiable fame. The Scots include Hamilton Brown, Napier, the two Cochranes, Fenton, the two Finlays, Gordon, Masson, Lord Charles Murray and the two Urquharts. The Irish include Blaquière, Church, Emerson, Fitz-Gibbon, Kirkpatrick, Hamilton, Castle, O'Fallon, Scanlan, Thomas, as well as one or both of the two Kennedys in the Ionian Islands. A similar proportion has already been seen among their supporters in England.[1] But although nationalism was already a force in Europe, these men were not nationalists. Like Napoleon and Byron, they were inspired by a motive which was above patriotism. Philhellenism was in a sense supra-nationalist, though a nation was what it helped to produce.

Byron's philhellenism survived in Church and Finlay, Gordon and Masson, and half a dozen others. It survived longest and in some ways most characteristically in Trelawny, the Celtic buccaneer, though he never returned to Greece after his escape from death in Odysseus' cave. He outlived them all, so far as the fate of the rest is known. In 1881, at the age of eighty-nine, he regretted that he could not go to South Africa to take part in the first Boer War. That was the last year of his life, but he had had a good run. To have presided at the cremation of Shelley's corpse, to have lived with Byron in Mesolonghi, to have married Odysseus' sister, to have survived an attempt at murder, to have written a best-selling novel, to have inspired Byron's *The Corsair* in his youth, to have been depicted by Millais as a buccaneer in *The North-West Passage* in his old age, to

[1] See p. 77 above.

have been commemorated after his death by Swinburne as "world-wide liberty's lifelong lover": these were not insignificant Adventures of a Younger Son. But with his death in 1881 philhellenism also died. It did not rise from the dead again, in a form that Byron and Trelawny would have recognised, until more than half a century later, when yet another war of independence had to be fought and won.

Epilogue

In temperament and ideology the philhellenes were predictable: radical, romantic, adventurous, quarrelsome, generous and mostly sincere. They were individualists who liked to be on their own, just as the romantic poets who spoke for them drew their inspiration from solitude. Their backgrounds reflected the social divisions of the age. There were men from the best families, the best regiments, and the best schools and universities (particularly Cambridge); at the other extreme were the seamen and artificers; and in between the middle-class professionals. Their social background, at least in the upper levels, reflected the composition of the London Greek Committee which supported them; but their professions did not. Predominant in the field were officers of the army and navy who had been deprived of active occupation by the end of the Napoleonic Wars, or else by their own incompatibility with their superiors and colleagues. Besides these, there was a mixed bag: several doctors, a schoolmaster, a merchant sea-captain, a handful of wandering scholars. But of the lawyers, parliamentarians, businessmen, economists and other learned professionals who formed the London Greek Committee, there were none in the field; nor did a single one of the classical antiquarians who thronged Greece in the first two decades of the century return to fight in the War of Independence.

There was in fact very little common membership between the three groups who fill the successive stages of this story: the travellers before 1821, the London Greek Committee, and the philhellenes in the field. Hobhouse and Knight belonged to the first and second; Church to the first and third; Stanhope and Blaquière to the second and third; Byron and Gordon alone to all three. It was not in keeping with the spirit of the age that scholars and grandees, or merchants and lawyers, should involve themselves directly in subversive activities and guerrilla warfare, even if they might encourage it from a distance. That was one of the differences between the philhellenes of the 1820s and those of the 1940s, whose experiences were in other ways so similar. It was also one of the differences which set Byron apart from his contemporaries. His personality alone dissolved the social barriers, bridged the gulf between London and Mesolonghi, and fused a common inspiration for philosophic liberals and "doing men". By way of fellow-poets in France and Italy, Germany and even Russia, his influence also reached out across a quarter of the century to the nationalist revolutions of 1848. Even the Chartists in England owed something to Byron and the philhellenes. David Urquhart knew it when he sought to spread Russophobe propaganda among the working classes; so did General Sir Charles James Napier when he refused to shoot them down.

The same influence reached across 120 years to revive philhellenism in another war of independence. This time it was the Greeks themselves, as carriers of the Byronic germ, who started the revival. Every experience of the 1820s was then repeated, including torture, betrayal and attempted murder, but also including loyalty, generosity and heroic self-sacrifice. The very names were the same, even if they were only pseudonyms: Odysseus, Kolokotronis, Botsaris, Karaiskakis, even Byron – all were there again in the 1940s. So were the many nationalities – British, American, Polish, Italian, Danish, and others whose presence would have delighted Byron's heart: a Palestinian Arab, a Jew from Aden, a Turkish Cypriot, a son of an Indian father and a Scottish mother. The British race was even more diversely represented than in Byron's day, with the usual contingents of Scots and Irish and Americans, but also New Zealanders, Australians, Rhodesians and South Africans. Between 1941 and 1945, the mountain headquarters of the Greek resistance boasted a Scottish adjutant, an explosives officer who learned his trade in the I.R.A., and as chief signals officers, in succession, an Irish Catholic from New

Zealand and a Channel Islander. Byron would not have noticed the difference; but he would have noticed, not without pleasure, a new feature of 20th-century philhellenism: the classical antiquarians were no longer aloof tourists, but in the forefront of the field.

There were other differences too. The 20th-century philhellenes were almost to a man civilians in uniform; and even the few professionals had not had to resign their commissions or get themselves cashiered in order to fight. There were therefore fewer adventurers and less romantic eccentricity, though still some of both. More important, because the war of independence in this century was part of an all-embracing crusade against a single diabolical enemy, it had fewer extraneous links with other miscellaneous symptoms of protest than the philhellenism of the 19th century. Nothing comparable to the progressive causes of the 1820s—Catholic emancipation, parliamentary reform, republicanism, utilitarianism, evangelicalism, abolition of slavery, freedom of trade unions, education for the working class, and so on—existed in the 1940s to be merged with philhellenism in a "protest movement", as it is called today.

There were other struggles in the background, it is true: between royalists and republicans in Greece, and between Communism and democracy in the western world of which Greece was a part. Greece has also become involved in later years with the "protest movement" through the cold war: "political prisoners", rocket bases and the military dictatorship have all helped to bring the Greeks into the forefront of ideological conflict. But all these developments are posterior to the philhellenism of the 20th century. None of these extraneous causes brought a single British parachutist to Greece between 1941 and 1945. The desire to liberate the Greeks from Nazi tyranny was not, as the desire to liberate them from the Ottoman Empire had been, part of a complex of radical ideas. It was in fact singularly free from ideology.

Nevertheless the philhellenes whom more than a century separated would have recognised each other. They would also have recognised each other's Greeks; and they would have acknowledged Byron, of course, as their common inspiration. He taught us all that "it were better to die doing something than nothing", Happy were those who did not have to die in learning it.

Bibliography

A. PRIMARY SOURCES

(i) Travels before the War of Independence.

Anon: *A Narrative in two parts: written in 1812* (London, 1813).

Anon: *Narrative of a Tour through Some Parts of the Turkish Empire* (London, 1829).

E. Blaquière: *Letters from the Mediterranean* (two vols., London, 1813).

John Bramsen: *Travels in Egypt, Syria, Cyprus, the Morea, Greece, Italy, etc., etc.* (two vols., London, 1820).

J. D. Carlyle: *Poems, Suggested Chiefly by Scenes in Asia Minor, Syria and Greece* (London, 1805).

E. D. Clarke: *Travels in Various Countries of Europe, Asia and Africa* (six vols., Cambridge, 1810–23).

C. R. Cockerell: *Travels in Southern Europe and the Levant, 1810–17* (ed. S. P. Cockerell; London, 1903).

Louise Demont: *Journal of the Visit of Her Majesty the Queen to Tunis, Greece and Palestine* (translated from the French; London, 1821).

Edward Dodwell: *A Classical and Topographical Tour through Greece* (London, 1819).

Hon. Frederick Sylvester Douglas: *An Essay on Certain Points of Resemblance between the Ancient and Modern Greeks* (London, 1813).

William Eton: *A Survey of the Turkish Empire* (London, 1798).

John Fuller: *Narrative of a Tour through Some Parts of the Turkish Empire* (London, 1830).

John Galt: *Voyages and Travels in the Years 1809, 1810 and 1811* (London, 1812).

John Galt: *Letters from the Levant* (London, 1813).

William Gell: *The Topography of Troy* (London, 1804).

William Gell: *The Geography and Antiquities of Ithaca* (London, 1807).

Sir William Gell: *Itinerary of the Morea* (London, 1817).

Sir William Gell: *The Itinerary of Greece* (London, 1819).

Sir William Gell: *Narrative of a Journey in the Morea* (London, 1823).

William Haygarth: *Greece—A Poem in three parts* (London, 1814).

J. C. Hobhouse: *A Journey through Albania and Other Provinces of Turkey in Europe and Asia to Constantinople during the Years 1809 and 1810* (2nd ed., two vols., London, 1813).

Henry Holland: *Travels in the Ionian Isles, Albania, Thessaly, Macedonia, etc., during the Years 1812 and 1813* (London, 1815).

Rev. T. S. Hughes: *Travels in Greece and Albania* (2nd ed., two vols., London, 1830).

T. R. Jolliffe: *Narrative of an Excursion from Corfu to Smyrna* (London, 1827).

Rev. William Jowett: *Christian Researches in the Mediterranean, from 1815 to 1820* (London, 1822).

Tertius T. C. Kendrick: *The Ionian Islands* (London, 1822).

John Macdonald Kinneir: *Journey through Asia Minor, Armenia and Koordistan* (London, 1818).

P. E. Laurent: *Recollections of a Classical Tour through Various Parts of Greece, Turkey and Italy, made in the Years 1818 and 1819* (London, 1821).

W. M. Leake: *Travels in the Morea* (two vols., London, 1830).

W. M. Leake: *Travels in Northern Greece* (four vols., London, 1835).

W. M. Leake: *Peloponnesiaca* (London, 1846).

Lady Hester Stanhope: *Travels, 1810–1817* (London, 1846).

John Turner: *Journal of a Tour in the Levant* (three vols., London, 1820).

Rev. Robert Walpole: *Memoir Relating to the European and Asiatic Turkey and Other Countries of the East* (London, 1818)

Rev. Robert Walpole: *Travels in Various Countries of the East* (London, 1820).
C. Wilkinson: *A Tour through Asia Minor and the Greek Islands* (London, 1806).
H. W. Williams: *Travels in Italy, Greece and the Ionian Islands* (two vols., Edinburgh, 1820).
William Rae Wilson: *Travels in Egypt and the Holy Land—the second edition: with a journey through Turkey, Greece, the Ionian Isles, Sicily, Spain, etc.* (London, 1824).
Joseph Woods: *Letters of an Architect from France, Italy, and Greece* (two vols., London, 1828).

(ii) During the War of Independence.

Edward Blaquière: *The Greek Revolution; its Origins and Progress* (London, 1824).
Edward Blaquière: *Narration of a Second Visit to Greece* (two vols., London, 1825).
Lord Broughton (J. C. Hobhouse): *Recollections of a Long Life* (six vols., London, 1909–12).
H. Lytton Bulwer: *An Autumn in Greece* (London, 1826).
Lord Byron: *Letters and Journals*, vol. VI (edited by Rowland E. Prothero; London, 1901).
Rev. R. Chatfield: *An Appeal to the British Public in the Cause of the Persecuted Greeks* (London, 1822); and *A Further Appeal* (London, 1823).
George Cochrane: *Wanderings in Greece* (two vols., London, 1837).
Sir Edward Codrington: *Compressed Narrative of the Proceedings of Vice-Admiral Sir Edward Codrington, During his Command of His Majesty's Ships and Vessels on the Mediterranean Station from the 28th of February 1827, until the 22nd of August 1828* (London, 1832).
Earl of Dundonald (Lord Cochrane): *Autobiography of a Seaman*, completed in the *Life* by his son, the eleventh Earl (London, 1860–61).
James Emerson, Count Pecchio, W. H. Humphreys: *A Picture of Greece in 1825*, (two vols., London, 1826).

James Emerson: *Letters from the Aegean* (two vols., London, 1829).

Lord Erskine: *An Appeal to the People of Great Britain on the Subject of Confederated Greece* (London, 1824).

George Finlay: *The Greek Revolution* (vols. VI–VII of *A History of Greece from its Conquest by the Romans to the Present Time, 146* B.C. *to* A.D. *1864*; ed. Rev. H. F. Tozer; Oxford., 1877).

P. Gamba: *The Narrative of Lord Byron's Last Journey to Greece* (London, 1825).

J. Gennadius (editor): *The Correspondence of Captain G. Hamilton* (London, 1930).

T. Gordon: *History of the Greek Revolution* (two vols., Edinburgh, 1832).

P. J. Green: *Sketches of the War in Greece* (London, 1827).

Frank A. Hastings: *Memoir on the Use of Shells, Hot Shot, and Carcass-Shells from Ship Artillery* (London, 1828).

Dr. S. G. Howe: *Letters and Journals* (ed. Laura E. Richards, two vols., Boston, 1906–1909).

Dr. S. G. Howe: *Historical Sketch*, vol. I (ed. George G. Arnakis; Austin, Texas, 1966).

Rev. T. S. Hughes: *An Address to the People of England in the Cause of the Greeks, Occasioned by the Late Inhuman Massacres in the Isle of Scio* (London, 1822).

Rev. T. S. Hughes: *Considerations Upon the Greek Revolution* (London, 1823).

W. H. Humphreys: *Journal of a Visit to Greece* (vol. II of *A Picture of Greece in 1825;* London, 1826).

George Jarvis: *His Journal and Related Documents* (ed. G. G. Arnakis, Thessaloniki, 1965).

Dr. James Kennedy: *Conversations on Religion with Lord Byron* (London, 1830).

A. Louriottes: *Correspondence Respecting the Steam Vessels* (London, 1827).

Edward Masson: *Philhellenika* (London, 1852).

Thomas Medwin: *Journal of the Conversations of Lord Byron* (London, 1824).

Julius Millingen: *Memoirs of the Affairs of Greece* (London, 1831).
Thomas Moore: *The Life of Lord Byron* (London, 1830).
Dr. Christian Müller: *Journey through Greece and the Ionian Islands, in June, July and August, 1821* (London, 1822).
William Parry: *The Last Days of Lord Byron* (London, 1825).
Hon. Col. Leicester Stanhope: *Greece in 1823 and 1824* (London, 1824).
Rev. Charles Swan: *Journal of a Voyage up the Mediterranean* (two vols., London, 1826).
E. J. Trelawny: *Adventures of a Younger Son* (London, 1835).
E. J. Trelawny: *Recollections of the Last Days of Shelley and Byron* (London, 1858).
D. Urquhart: *The Spirit of the East* (two vols., London, 1833).
George Waddington: *A Visit to Greece in 1823 and 1824* (London, 1825).

(iii) After the War of Independence.

Thomas Alcock: *Travels in Russia, Persia, Turkey and Greece in 1828–9* (London, 1831).
Rufus Anderson: *Observations upon the Peloponnesus and Greek Islands made in 1829* (Boston, 1830).
Anon: *Sketches in Greece and Turkey* (London, 1833).
John Carne: *Letters from the East* (two vols., London, 1830).
E. M. Church: *Sir Richard Church in Italy and Greece* (Edinburgh, 1895).
Sir Richard Church: *Observations on an Eligible Line of Frontier for Greece as an Independent State* (London, 1830).
Hon. W. E. Fitzmaurice: *A Cruise to Egypt, Palestine, and Greece during Five Months' Leave of Absence* (London, 1834).
Capt. Charles Colville Frankland: *Travels to and from Constantinople in the Years 1827 and 1828* (two vols., London, 1829).
Edward A. Freeman: *The Ottoman Power in Europe, its Nature, its Growth and its Decline* (London, 1877).

Edward Giffard: *A Short Visit to the Ionian Islands, Athens, and the Morea* (London, 1837).

Major-General T. Gordon: *Account of Two Visits to the Anopaea or Highlands above Thermopylae made in June and July 1837* (Athens, 1838).

Rev. John Hartley: *Researches in Greece and the Levant* (London, 1831).

Francis Hervé: *A Residence in Greece and Turkey* (two vols., London, 1837).

Major the Hon. George Keppel: *Narrative of a Journey Across the Balcan* (two vols., London, 1831).

A. W. Kinglake: *Eothen* (London, 1844).

William Knight: *Oriental Outlines* (London, 1838).

Edward Lear: *Journals of a Landscape Painter in Albania etc.* (London, 1851).

Richard Monckton Milnes: *Memorials of a Tour in Some Parts of Greece, Chiefly Poetical* (London, 1834).

Col. Charles James Napier: *The Colonies: Treating of their Value Generally—of the Ionian Islands in Particular* (London, 1833).

Robert Pashley: *Travels in Crete* (two vols., Cambridge. 1837).

Adolphus Slade: *Records of Travels in Turkey, Greece etc.* (two vols., London, 1831).

Adolphus Slade: *Turkey, Greece and Malta* (two vols., London, 1837).

Capt. T. Abercromby Trant: *Narrative of a Journey through Greece in 1830* (London, 1830).

Aubrey de Vere: *Picturesque Sketches of Greece and Turkey* (London, 1850).

Charles K. Tuckerman: *The Greeks of Today* (New York, 1878).

Rev. R. Walsh: *A Residence at Constantinople* (two vols., London, 1836).

E. C. Wines: *Two Years and a Half in the American Navy*, vol. II (London, 1833).

Christopher Wordsworth: *Athens and Attica* (London, 1836).

Christopher Wordsworth: *Greece: Pictorial, Descriptive and Historical* (London, 1839).

B. SECONDARY SOURCES

(i) Relating to Greek affairs.

Lady Bourchier: *Memoir of the Life of Admiral Sir Edward Codrington* (two vols., London, 1873).

C. W. Crawley: *The Question of Greek Independence, 1821–1833* (Cambridge, 1930).

Douglas Dakin: *British and American Philhellenes During the Greek War of Independence, 1821–1833* (Thessaloniki, 1955).

Douglas Dakin: *British Intelligence of Events in Greece, 1824–1827* (Athens, 1959).

Domna Dontas: *The Last Phase of the War of Independence in Western Greece, 1827–1829* (Thessaloniki, 1966).

Z. D. Ferriman: *Some English Philhellenes* (London, 1917).

Sir Richard Jebb: *Modern Greece, with papers on Byron in Greece, etc.* (London, 1880).

Stephen A. Larrabee: *Hellas Observed—The American Experience of Greece, 1775–1865* New York, 1957).

H. A. Lidderdale (editor and translator): *The Memoirs of General Makriyannis, 1797–1864* (London, 1966).

Doris Langley Moore: *The Late Lord Byron* (London, 1961).

J. E. Morpurgo: *The Last Days of Shelley and Byron* (being the complete text of Trelawny's "Recollections" edited with additions from contemporary sources; London, 1952).

Harold Nicolson: *Byron—The Last Journey* (London, 1924).

Harold Nicolson: *Small Talk* (London, 1937).

Iris Origo: *The Last Attachment* (London, 1949).

William St. Clair: *Lord Elgin and the Marbles* (Oxford, 1967).

T. B. Spencer: *Fair Greece Sad Relic* (London, 1954).

Warren Tute: *Cochrane—A Life of Admiral the Earl of Dundonald* (London, 1965).

C. E. Vulliamy: *Byron* (London, 1948).

Timothy Ware: *The Orthodox Church* (London, 1963).

Shirley Howard Weber: *Voyages and Travels in the Near East made During the XIX Century* (Princeton, 1952).

C. M. Woodhouse: *The Greek War of Independence* (London, 1952).
C. M. Woodhouse: *The Battle of Navarino* (London, 1965).
C. M. Woodhouse: *The Story of Modern Greece* (London, 1968).

(ii) General History.

M. S. Anderson: *The Eastern Question* (London, 1966).
Asa Briggs: *The Age of Improvement* (London, 1960).
J. H. Clapham: *An Economic History of Modern Britain* (three vols., Cambridge 1926–38).
T. K. Derry and T. L. Jarman: *The Making of Modern Britain* (London 1956).
H. A. R. Gibb and H. Bowen: *Islamic Society and the West* (London, 1950–57).
Edward Vose Gulick: *Europe's Classical Balance of Power* (New York, 1955).
Élie Halévy: *A History of the English People in the Nineteenth Century* (translated from the French; London, 1949): vol. I: *England in 1815;* vol. II: *The Liberal Awakening, 1815–1830.*
E. J. Hobsbawm: *The Age of Revolution* (London, 1962).
Graham Hough: *The Romantic Poets* (London, 1953).
R. B. Mowat: *A History of European Diplomacy, 1815–1914* (London, 1922).
New Cambridge Modern History, vol. IX (Cambridge, 1965).
J. H. Plumb: *England in the Eighteenth Century, 1714–1851* (London, 1950).
George Rudé: *Revolutionary Europe, 1783–1815* (London, 1964).
H. W. V. Temperley: *The Foreign Policy of Canning, 1822–27* (London, 1926).
David Thomson: *England in the Nineteenth Century* (London, 1950).
C. K. Webster: *The Foreign Policy of Castlereagh, 1812–15* (two vols., London, 1925–31).

Appendix I

British volunteers active in Greece[1] during the War of Independence, 1821–29

Captain Thomas Bannister
Dr. Bentham
William Billet
— Blackett
Edward Blaquière
James Bossen
Dr. Alexander Boutron
Dr. Henry J. Bradfield
J. Hamilton Brown
Dr. Bryce
H. Lytton Bulwer
Lieut. Bushel
Lord Byron
Captain Francis T. Castle
Captain Castlebone
General Sir Richard Church
Lieut. George S. Cochrane
Lord Cochrane
Captain Thomas S. Crosby
Captain George Darby
Lieut. Downing (*alias* Kirkwood)
James Emerson

[1] Dakin, *British and American Philhellenes*, pp. 243–5.

Captain William Fenton
George Finlay
Kirkman Finlay
Lieut. Gibbon Fitz-Gibbon
— Fowke
Charles Freeston
Henry Frellsun
Lieut. Edgar Garston
Dr. Gally
— Gill
Dr. Goffy
General Thomas Gordon
James Hall
Ralph Hall
Captain John Hane
Captain Frank Abney Hastings
Richard Henry
Captain Henry Hesketh
William Higginson
— Hodges
Captain William H. Humphreys
Lieut. George B. Hutchings (*alias* Captain St. George)
— Hyler
Lieut. Edward Jermyn
Dr. Johnson
John Jones
— Kendrew
Captain Francis Kirkpatrick
George Lee
Captain Lutchins
Captain Lypton
William Martin
Lieut. Morris Moore
Lord Charles Murray
Captain Charles O'Fallon

Alfred Parry
William Parry
Captain Payne
Lieut. Peppercorn
Dr. John Quail
James Ratcliffe
James Robertson
John Rosbreck
William Russell
John Ryan
Lieut. William Scanlan
Colonel the Hon. Leicester Stanhope
— Stellway
Robert James Tennent
Captain George Thomas
James Thompson
Dr. Tindall
Edward John Trelawny
Lieut. David Urquhart
Colonel Charles Gordon Urquhart
Captain H. G. Whitcombe
Arthur Gower Winter

Appendix II

Members of the London Greek Committee[1]

E. H. Barker
S. M. Barratt, M.P.
Barber Beaumont
The Hon. H. G. Bennet, M.P.
Jeremy Bentham
Samuel Boddington
John Bowring
Henry Brougham, M.P.
Sir F. Burdett, Bart., M.P.
Lord Byron
Robert Campbell
Thomas Campbell
Robert Chaloner, M.P.
Dr. Chatfield
John Christie
The Rev. Dr. Adam Clark
T. W. Coke, M.P.
S. Crompton, M.P.
Lord Dacre
Colonel T. H. Davies, M.P.
The Hon. Captain George Dundas
Lord Ebrington, M.P.
Edward Ellice, M.P.

[1] *The Nineteenth Century*, vol. C (September 1926), p. 398n.

Colonel Sir Howard Elphinstone
C. A. Elton of Clifton
Lord Erskine
William Evans, M.P.
Lord Fitzwilliam
J. B. Gilchrist
Thomas Gordon of Cairness
Lord Archibald Hamilton, M.P.
James Henry
Sir Robert Heron
J. C. Hobhouse, M.P.
Joseph Hume, M.P.
The Hon. H. C. Hely-Hutchinson, M.P.
Colonel Jones
The Hon. Douglas Kinnaird
H. G. Knight
The Hon. Sir Robert Lawrence
J. G. Lambton, M.P.
Dr. Lemprière of Shaldon
T. Barrett-Lennard, M.P.
General Long
Zachary Macaulay
Sir James Mackintosh, M.P.
Dr. Maclean
The Rev. Dr. M'Crie
J. Mavrocordatos
J. Maxwell, M.P.
Lord Milton, M.P.
J. B. Monck, M.P.
Thomas Moore
Lord Nugent, M.P.
William Ord, M.P.
Samuel Parkes
The Rev. Dr. Parr of Hatton
Sir T. D. Paul, Bart.

Sir W. Paxton
George Philips, M.P.
H. Pierce
N. Ralli
D. Ricardo, M.P.
T. S. Rice, M.P.
Samuel Rogers
Charles Rumbold, M.P.
Lord John Russell, M.P.
James Scarlett, M.P.
D. Schinas
John Smith, M.P.
William Smith, M.P.
Lord Sondes
The Hon. Colonel Leicester Stanhope
D. Sykes, M.P.
Richard Taylor
The Marquess of Titchfield
Henry Tulk
William Turnbull
General Weatherstone
W. W. Whitmore, M.P.
John Wilks
J. Williams, M.P.
W. Williams, M.P.
Sir Robert Wilson, M.P.
Sir Matthew Wood, M.P.

Index

(N.B. Names which are listed only in the Appendices are not included in the Index.)